FINDING FAITH

in the FACE *of* DOUBT

For Marion & Jane Emerson—
With all good wishes!
Joe Willis

FINDING FAITH

in the FACE *of* DOUBT

A Guide for Contemporary Seekers

JOSEPH S. WILLIS

Quest Books
Theosophical Publishing House

Wheaton, Illinois ♦ Chennai (Madras), India

The Theosophical Society wishes to acknowledge the generous support of the Kern Foundation in the publication of this book.

First Quest Edition 2001

The Theosophical Publishing House
P. O. Box 270
Wheaton, IL 60189-0270

Library of Congress Cataloging-in-Publication Data

Willis, Joseph S.
Finding faith in the face of doubt: a guide for contemporary seekers /
Joseph S. Willis
    p. cm.
Includes bibliographical references.
ISBN 0-8356-0805-0
1. Agnosticism.   2. Apologetics.   I. Title.

BL2747.2. W55 2001
291.2—dc21   2001041640

        5   4   3   2   1   *   01   02   03   04   05   06

Printed in the United States of America

*With deepest love to my two youngest grandchildren,
Ariel Holmes and Hunter Holmes,
an exceedingly precious part of my old age.*

If a man will begin with certainties, he shall end in doubts;
but if he will be content to begin with doubts,
he shall end in certainties.

—Francis Bacon

Grateful acknowledgment is made for permission to reprint copyrighted material:

Campbell, Joseph, with Bill Moyers. *The Power of Myth*. Doubleday, 1988. Used by permission of Doubleday, a division of Random House, Inc.

Capra, Fritjof. *The Web of Life: A New Understanding of Living Systems*. New York: Anchor Books, Doubleday, 1996. Used by permission of Doubleday, a division of Random House, Inc.

From *The Tao of Physics* by Fritjof Capra. © 1975, 1983, 1991, 1999 by Fritjof Capra. Reprinted by arrangement with Shambhala Publications, Inc., Boston, www.shambhala.com

Ellsberg, Robert, ed. *Gandhi on Christianity*. Maryknoll, N.Y.: Orbis Books, 1991. Used by permission of Orbis Books.

Fletcher, Joseph. *Situation Ethics*. Philadelphia: Westminster Press, 1966. Used by permission.

Fredriksen, Paula. *From Jesus to Christ: Origins of the New Testament Images of Jesus*. Yale University Press, 1988. Used by permission of Yale University Press Publications.

Harrison, Edward. *Masks of the Universe*. New York: McGraw Hill, 1985. Used by permission of Edward Harrison.

Excerpted from *The Soul's Code* (Random House) by James Hillman. © 1966 by James Hillman, reprinted by permission of Melanie Jackson Agency, L.L.C.

Kerenyi, Carl. *Asklepios: Archetypal Image of the Physician's Existence*. Copyright © 1959 by Princeton University Press. Reprinted by permission of Princeton University Press.

Krutch, Joseph Wood. *The Measure of Man*. Peter Smith Publisher, Inc., Gloucester, MA, 1978. Used by permission of Peter Smith Publisher, Inc.

Every effort has been made to secure permission for material quoted in this book. Any additional copyright holders are invited to contact the publisher so that proper credit can be given in future editions.

CONTENTS

In Appreciation

Through the years, by the process of living, I became who I am, but it was not an individual effort. I am, like everyone else, the result of a community upbringing. Hosts of people made contributions that I should but cannot reliably acknowledge. Parents, grandparents, teachers, friends, and many more deeply influenced my living and my understanding. Ideas from long-ago conversations still resonate in my mind, though only vaguely reminiscent of when and where they took place. Books gave me new insights; motion pictures and theatrical productions inspired; occasionally even sermons or speeches brought small transformations. Music enriched me both as I heard it and as I sang in a fine choir. My debt to many persons and events I cannot identify is great.

One special friend is the Rev. Robert Latham, who was the senior minister while I was associate minister at Jefferson Unitarian Church in Golden, Colorado. I found in Robert an intelligent colleague who generously encouraged me to try new ways of ministry and who shared in many conversations that helped to expand my vision.

When it comes to the production of this book, I must mention certain people whose actions set me on my way and helped me to keep moving ahead as I shared with them small portions of the growing manuscript. Their encouragement and critique were very important to me. Among these were friends in many places. One of the first to read early parts of the manuscript was Charles Newton of Del Mar, California, a retired communication consultant and my wife's cousin's husband. His critique was not exceptionally gentle, but it was cogent and honest, and it led me to rethink my presentation and write in a different way. Derrell and Mary Jean Gillingham of Albuquerque, New Mexico, gave support and encouragement as the ideas formed and finally found their way to the computer. Later on, my long-time friend, Rev. Ed Henderlite of Salem, Oregon, a retired United Church of Christ minister, gratified me with his positive comments about my approach to theology.

In the Denver area, several friends were deeply involved, mostly from Jefferson Unitarian Church. Marcie Mustoe and Jim Harvey were very responsive to initial fragments of chapters. I thank most deeply Barbara Bailey, who organized a virtual cheerleading squad of church members to read and respond to the early parts of the book. From them I gained confidence to move forward. Among these Unitarian friends were Dr. Stephanie Briggs, Beth Finnell, Dr. Stan Hamilton and Mary Hamilton, James Matera and Betty Lynn Ferguson, Chuck Mowry, and Dr. Tom Storm and Nancy Storm. They ventured careful evaluations and reactions to the manuscript and shared ideas about how to aim the book at a specific audience. Though he had only recently been called as senior minister of Jefferson Unitarian Church, Rev. Peter Morales was helpful in suggesting some practical steps in marketing the book. I also gratefully acknowledge the Rev. Dr. Charles Schuster, who invited me to share my evolving manuscript with the Friday Morning Theology Class of Arvada United Methodist Church. Rev. Schuster's dynamic leadership called on the wisdom and insights of these brave souls who assembled from seven to eight AM each week to discuss the book chapter by chapter. They honored me with their candid and forthright comments, which occasioned several significant revisions. I note with special gratitude Marsha Clark, whose razor-sharp mind and loving spirit challenged me to explain myself better; and Reese and Sally Ganster, who proofread the entire manuscript and offered ways of improving it.

My family—my daughters and son and their families—were all encouraging and supportive. These include Jodee Reynolds and my grandson Gene; Marsha Willis and her husband, Mark Lawson; Heidi Sexton; Scott Stockley and his wife, Karla; and Julie Holmes, whose husband, Shawn, assisted with mysterious processes on the Web. I am especially grateful to my daughter Marsha, who took time from her own book-publishing venture to read and respond with pertinent and encouraging suggestions.

But most of all, I must gratefully single out my wife, Nancy, who researched a great deal of information about possible publishers, handled a myriad of administrative details, and collected other information that was needed to get the book properly launched. In addition, she used her considerable editorial skills in proofreading the manuscript, and often, she very quietly and lovingly asked me, "But what are you trying to say here?" If Nancy did not understand, I knew I was not writing clearly! She felt equally free to say, "I think that is good." She was my best support, my severest critic, and my most generous source of encouragement.

My editor, Jane Lawrence, shared her high expertise in the most beneficial way! Finally, I rejoice to say that the staff at Quest Books has been unfailingly competent, considerate, and cooperative. I consider myself truly fortunate to be in relationship with Quest as this book is published. My indebtedness is real, and my gratitude is genuine.

A Note to the Reader

In reality, this book got a start when I was in high school and college in the 1930s, though I did not know it at the time. I enjoyed being part of the youth group in the church I attended. Particularly rewarding to me was taking part in summer conferences where, for a week, young people from two or three states gathered in a somewhat primitive camp in the cool mountains. We enjoyed classes, worship services, and times of thoughtfulness, as well as campfires and games, mostly in the beauty of the pine-scented open air. We formed deep friendships and felt stirrings of spirit (as well as some of the flesh!) as we learned together. I finally decided I would go into ministry—a sincere decision, though based mostly on deep emotion and much less on real comprehension.

However, as a major in biology, I was committed also to understanding what scientists were saying about life and the vast universe. If the cosmos inspired awe in me as a young man, I find it even more awesome today in light of the tremendous expansion of scientific knowledge since the days of my youth.

Even then I found occasional tension between the two parts of my life, and I hoped that theological school would lead to answers. However, my classes in seminary did not provide any closure, and years of working in churches simply made the struggle sharper. The dilemma led me to three more years of graduate theological study, during which I began to open doors to puzzling problems in my mind.

As time passed, I inevitably arrived at a critical juncture. Like Robert Frost's traveler facing diverging roads in the wood, I was "sorry I could not travel both and be one traveler." I resigned from church life and worked in the world of public education.

Years sped by and through an unplanned series of events, I

became a member and then a staff member of a different church. I found that my meandering search for a way to unify my life became a resource as I dealt with more and more adults who could no longer live with integrity because they doubted the substance of their old faith.

We became searchers together through personal conversation and discussion groups. I read widely, listened deeply, thought long. Sometimes discoveries came with an "Aha!" of recognition. Sometimes little trails opened that became wider paths and even broad highways. Through the years, people in my various adult classes, friends who had shared ideas with me, even family members, suggested that I write down my emerging ideas so that they could be shared more widely.

Finally, in my very late years, this book arose in what I call organic fashion. It *grew*—from class lectures, from handouts to students, and eventually from some tentative efforts to begin a manuscript. It now stands as an attempt to share an open faith that has been rewarding to me, and it offers support to the many other people who struggle with deep doubts about religious dogma. It is intended to aid the search for integrity of spirit and intellect. It is for those who wish to be able to keep in the same human mind both a respect for the methods and discoveries of science and the quest for an honest faith—a commitment centered in the Ultimate Mystery that many people call "God."

May the spirit of truth, the joy of freedom, and a sense of wonder flow through you as you travel a road similar to the one I have traveled for many years, and hope still to travel while my years yet have days.

Joe Willis
Arvada, Colorado
March 26, 2001

Introduction

This book is about faith and truth. Which is more important? That's like asking which side of a coin is more important; they can't be separated and each needs the other. So the book deals truthfully with faith, and it insists that you must have faith in truth. If you can't really believe in the truth of what your faith holds about the universe, your faith will crumble. In the words of Bishop John Shelby Spong's book, *Here I Stand*, "The heart cannot worship what the mind rejects."[1] On the other hand, human reason—the ability to create and analyze and see relationships—is the source of faith. No unreasoning being can have faith.

Everyone needs a faith, a commitment, that is congruent with her or his reason and knowledge, and it must be personal. There is no single way; ultimate truth is simply beyond human reach. But for yourself, for the sake of your own integrity, as a place upon which to stand as you make your life's decisions, you must find a faith that makes real sense to you. It's your life, your heart, and your mind. This book is for people who doubt the traditional answers, but who believe that the sheer accumulation of material things is not a satisfying way to live. It's about faith and reason and truth from science, philosophy, and the religions of humankind.

But now for a true story and a made-up story. (You can decide which is which!)

The professor who headed the philosophy department at the university where I was working as an interdenominational chaplain had just returned from a sabbatical. He had been gone for a year to study Buddhism in southern Asia. Now he was speaking to the group of students who gathered every Sunday night for a discussion on some aspect of religion.

He was trying to make clear the Buddhist approach to life. "So," he said, "they go on the basis, 'Seek not to desire anything too much, but do not desire too much not to desire too much.'" The students were amused at this idea, but they could understand what he meant. If you desire too much not to desire too much, you are already defeating yourself.

It was 2:30 AM and the woman sighed as she looked again at the clock, which seemed to be stuck or at best moving at half speed. Her mind was busy circling and recircling over the interview scheduled for the next morning. She thought again of the letter and resumé she had sent. It was a job she both wanted and needed, but had she expressed herself well in her letter? Was her resumé in order? Did she sound as if she were really competent?

Was there any way she could get some sleep? She knew she could not be alert unless she did. She sighed again and turned toward her husband, who stirred and asked sleepily, "Still can't sleep?"

"No," she said.

"Try to relax a bit," he said.

"I'm trying to relax," she said.

"Maybe that's the problem. Maybe you are trying too hard."

"Maybe," she said. "But how can I stop trying too hard?"

"Just try harder not to try so hard," he said.

Such paradoxes fill our lives, but we tend to overlook them because we omit one part of the paradox. It seems simpler that way, but that simpler way is simply wrong. Thus, we say, "Try to relax," but the whole statement should be, "Try to relax, but the harder you try, the less relaxed you will be!"

This book is very much about truth, but it is not all literally true. If the reader looks for literally factual reports of events and conversations, this is not a true book. There is some factual information in it, but many of the characters in the illustrative stories are not real people, though they could be almost anybody. The conversations in the book resemble conversations that I have enjoyed at different times with different people, but many of them never actually happened; they are not literally true.

However, the ideas that they contain are reasonably true representations of ideas by which I live, by which, in some sense, we all live, whether we know it or not. Nevertheless, if truth can be found only in factual accounts of actual events, then this book is not true. On the other hand, if you can accept that it is not literally factual you will be able to consider the truth that lies beyond the little fragments that we call facts.

"We hold these truths to be self-evident," says the Declaration of Independence of the United States, "that all men are created equal, that they are endowed by their creator with certain inalienable rights . . . among these are life, liberty, and the pursuit of happiness." This is an enumeration not of facts, but of truths, ideas, and ideals for which men and women were willing to fight and even to die.

This is not to say that facts are not related to truth. Facts, of course, are not facts unless they are true, and it is the nature of truth that it includes facts. Any larger truth must be in accordance with facts of what we know about the universe and ourselves. To ignore the facts would make such a truth untrue. Truth cannot contradict facts. For instance, if an 1840s abolitionist were to have said, "There are ten million black slaves in our nation," that would be a fact that could be affirmed or denied. But unless the truth—that it is wrong for human beings to own other human beings—is added to the numerical facts, there would be no motive to abolish slavery. By the same token, if there had been no slaves, the truth about the wrongness of slavery would have been irrelevant.

Facts, in general, do not provide the stuff from which a person can construct a motive for living. It may be a fact that there are, say, thirty-five million telephones in New York City (I have no idea what the correct figure is!), but such information gives neither motive nor direction for human life. Besides, facts are slippery. Even before a telephone book is published, the information it contains is inaccurate. Some listed subscribers are no longer living in the place where they are listed and they may not have phones, and new subscribers are on-line but not included in the book.

Thus, there are indeed some facts in that collection of books we call the Bible. But the meaning in the Bible is not essentially in whatever facts it contains, but in the truths that the words carry. People who hold that the Bible is true because it is essentially factual thereby condemn it to being false. For example, Jesus' parable of the Good Samaritan does not claim to be an account of an actual event; rather, it is an illustrative story to demonstrate a truth.

If, on the other hand, people reject the Bible because it is not purely factual, they are deaf to the truths that speak from its pages. By judging everything on factual accuracy, both the befuddled believer and the scoffing skeptic are disloyal to the search for truth. The paradox is that if you insist that the Bible is all factual, you make it false. If you can accept that it is not all literally factual, you free its truth to speak to you.

We face many paradoxes as we live our daily lives. This is most obvious when we think of the deepest truths by which we live—the basic assumptions that guide us. This book attempts to help us be aware of some of those paradoxes and to deal with them honestly. It is not anything like "Ten Steps to Making a Complete Value System," or "Five Ways to Know That You Are Always Right." Such lists are always too simple and contrived.

"We know that we do not know" is a central paradox. Another is, "You must choose even if you don't know what all the choices mean," or maybe it should be, "You cannot choose not to choose." Yet another is, "You can be free only if you choose to limit your freedom." Others will emerge in the context of daily life.

Some of the material presented here is simply a straightforward discussion of various issues. Some chapters contain conversations and encounters, but there is no attempt to assemble a plot. Like life itself, the book does not develop by strictly logical outlines, but grows organically as one thing leads to another. In reality, that is the way we build our own theologies: they grow; we do not design them.

Now and again I will quote various authors, but there are no footnotes. (There are endnotes and a list of resources at the back of the book.) This book is not a scholarly work; it is not for academics.

It is not for professional philosophers or professional theologians or professional ethicists. It is for intelligent people who seek ideas about how to face the contradictory events of life, who know how often life requires us to make choices when the alternatives are not clear. It is for people who want to be honest yet accept the paradoxes that none of us can avoid. It is for people who might acknowledge some kind of faith, but who cannot give assent to any creed because they know that every creed is at least partly wrong. It is for people who choose to live full and open lives, even as they know that they do not know all the answers.

Part One

A World *of* Paradox *and* Puzzle

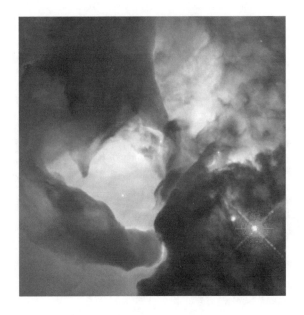

The truth is rarely pure and never simple.

—Oscar Wilde

The Case of the Faithful Agnostic

When I was a boy, the most powerful member of our family was my grandmother, who lived next door to us. I was about twelve or thirteen years old when I realized that everything our family did revolved around her. My mother was constantly taking her to the doctor, buying her groceries, cleaning her house, bringing meals to her. If my mother and father wanted to take us three kids for a rare weekend trip to the mountains, it all had to be checked out first with Grandma. Could she be left for three days? Could she go along for the little vacation?

My grandfather also, when he got home from work, first attended to her before he went out and worked in his yard. I wondered how she acquired so much power over us. It finally dawned on me: she was so powerful because she was so weak! Her continuing illnesses were the source of her strength. I had discovered paradox, though at the time I did not know the name for it.

The World of Paradox

A paradox is a statement that seems to say opposite things: "She was strong because of her weakness." I am not implying that she was not really ill, though I think she magnified her illness and was preoccupied with her ailments. In any case, she took advantage of her disabilities and of her family. My brother and I and our younger sister came to resent it.

Life is full of paradoxes.

- Some people work very hard to avoid work.

- Some people are smart enough to pretend to be less smart, and thus avoid responsibility.

- Some people seem to enjoy being unhappy.

- Some people are overly proud of their humility.

Sometimes when I am asked what my theological position is, I often—and paradoxically—call myself a faithful agnostic. I say it quite seriously, though I enjoy the consternation it sometimes produces.

Matt, a young man in one of my classes, was almost angry at my words. "A faithful agnostic is a—what do you call it? An oxymoron? That's like an honest thief or a gentle bully or a brave coward. In real life, you can't be two opposite things at the same time!"

"But you can," I insisted. "Suppose I was forty-five years old and said I wanted to join the kindergarten class in the charter school. They would say I was too old, and of course I would have to agree with that. But then I might say that since I seemed to be too old, maybe I should start drawing on my retirement plan next year. Then they would say that I was too young. I would be too old and too young at the same time, wouldn't I? Or suppose that I wanted to be a jockey and ride a racehorse; they would say I was too big. If I agreed to settle for being a tackle on a professional football team, they would say I was too small. I would be too big and too small at the same time."

"Yes," he objected, "but that is only because you are talking about two different situations: you can't be too big and too small at the same time about the same thing. So how can you be agnostic and have faith at the same time?"

"That's not too tough," I said, "though it is a little subtle. To be agnostic means you don't know whether a thing is true or not; you don't know for sure that God exists, or that there is life after death, or whatever. Right?" He nodded in agreement.

"Okay. So now, what does it mean to be faithful?"

"Well," he said, "it means you can be depended on. And it also means you believe in something. You believe in some ideas, some religion, some kind of theological stuff."

"All right," I responded. "Matt, you didn't want me to say I could be different things at the same time, but you are saying that *faithful* means two different things at the same time. And that's okay; I agree with that. I am just pointing it out. But which one do you want to talk about when you say I can't be a faithful agnostic?"

"I was thinking mostly of believing something," he responded. "'I have faith in God' is different from 'I am agnostic about God.' How can you believe in something if you don't know whether or not it exists?"

Faith vs. Knowledge

Having faith in something is not the same as knowing it. For instance, you know that your doctor has many skills, and you even know what some of them are. Also, she has skills that you don't know about. What you do know is that she is a competent and caring person. You trust her integrity and honesty and that she will do the right thing to the utmost of her knowledge.

Now suppose that your doctor tells you to see a certain specialist for a complete diagnosis. You don't know anything about the other doctor, and you don't know much about the cause of your own health problem. Nevertheless, you would probably go see the specialist and follow his recommendation for treatment even if there were no guarantee of a successful outcome.

That is a good example of faith. Faith is not just agreeing to a set of propositions or saying a creed. If you recited a phrase or two, such as, "I believe that my doctor is trustworthy," and "My doctor recommends this specialist," or "I believe that the specialist is competent," but then refused to see the specialist, that would not show faith. The decision to trust your welfare, maybe even your life, to that person's skills is an act of faith.

The great theologian Paul Tillich says that faith is the state of being ultimately concerned.[2] I take this to mean, in part, that the fundamental idea on which you base your perception of the universe is the idea from which all your actions and reactions flow. If you commit yourself to the idea that the Ultimate Reality is, for you, a personal loving God, you will think and act one way. If, on the other hand, you conclude that the Ultimate Reality is the physical universe itself, then you will think and act another way. From your ultimate commitment all subsequent commitments flow. If success is your ultimate value, then you will devote your life's energy toward serving success. If your nation is your central value, then you will devote your energies to the service of the nation.

The agnostic does not know whether God exists or if prayer does any good or if God has a plan. In fact, *what she knows is that she does not know.* Can a person build a faith on that? How is that related to ultimate commitment? I start with my own experience as a faithful agnostic. Of course, this is not the exact process I actually went through, for it was not a one-time series of logical steps. It developed slowly through time. However, I reconstruct it this way in order to make sense of it. First, I asked myself, is there anything beyond the physical universe? Before I answered, I needed to clarify the question. Does "beyond the universe" mean other universes outside the one we belong to? Or does it mean some sort of source, some sort of Creator, something that holds it together?

But I want to be honest and not play tricks with words. I looked at a few other questions. What enables the universe (or universes) to exist? If there were more than one, do the same laws govern them all? How can we find that out? If there were other universes completely outside ours, we would have no way to learn about them. And if they were connected, they would form a single, much bigger universe.

I also must remember that the universe is not just physical matter like galaxies and stars and planets and clouds of gas. Whatever laws make it work are part of the universe too, so the universe is also forces and energy. It is gravity, the strong force and the weak force, and the processes that determine how energies flow, and all the rest of it. That raises other questions: Did the universe itself make the physical laws by which it works? Or were they already there when the universe began? Before space and time began, where was "there"? Are universal laws self-existent whether the universe exists or not? Do they operate in all universes—if there are other universes? I found even the questions mysterious, and I surely did not know the answers!

Where Did God Come From?

People who believe in the biblical Creator believe that whatever laws operate in the universe came from God. Back when I believed that God was a person, I thought that the answer to all such questions had to be, "God did it." That one act of faith, believing in God as Creator, simply answered all the questions and avoided the unanswerable. I came to realize, however, that there was still a question that loomed beyond this affirmation. It is a question that is usually asked by little children, but when I got older, I asked it again. "Where did God come from?"

The answer is, "There is no answer," which brings us to the ultimate mystery: What was there before there was anything? How could anything, even God, be without beginning? What was it like before creation? Was there any time when there was no universe? If time began with the universe, could there be any before-time-existed? Such questions lead us into mysteries that we can't know, questions that we can't answer. I realized that thinking about God brought me into more levels of mystery.

Now let us suppose that there is nothing beyond the universe. What if the Big Bang didn't come from anything? If the principles and laws originated with the universe, then the universe itself is the Ultimate Reality, and there is nothing beyond it. That would mean that the universe produced whatever it was that suddenly expanded in the Big Bang and became the universe. But how could it produce what was there before it began? How could it start its own beginning? That also is very mysterious. But after all, that's why I'm an agnostic! In a real sense, we all have to be agnostic when we deal with the idea of the Ultimate.

Edward Harrison, Professor of Physics and Astronomy at the University of Massachusetts, writes of the Big Bang in his book, *Masks of the Universe*. He says that if we follow the best theories back to a time about one ten-million-trillion-trillion-trillionth of a second after the beginning, "we can go no farther. An orderly historical sequence of events has ceased to exist, and past and future have become meaningless. Here, in the realm of quantum cosmology—the chaosmos—lie the secrets that foretell the future of the universe."[3]

If a person holds that the universe is the Ultimate Reality, that there is nothing beyond the universe, she confronts a mystery that our logic and reason cannot penetrate. And he who believes that God created the universe still faces unknown mysteries. He bets his life that there is a Creator, but to say that "God did it," is still to say that the start of it all is beyond our comprehension. God is the greatest of all mysteries.

Sometimes people claim to know too much about God. They have the Ultimate Reality outlined like a term paper, with roman numerals and capital letters and numbered subparagraphs. That kind of carefully organized Ultimate Reality is a creation of the human mind, not the great mysterious Ground of Everything. A thoughtful person cannot have much confidence in a God who is too clearly defined. The human mind has great difficulty in comprehending the physical universe itself, let alone the mystery that shrouds the Ultimate!

I bet my life on the reality of the mystery. I am confident that whatever processes empowered the beginning of the universe are beyond any human explanation. (By the way, our word *confident* means "with faith.") So I do have faith that the Ultimate is a mystery, and I also have faith that it is not given to human beings to understand that mystery, though future discoveries may shed more light on it. New bits of knowledge are unveiled as science moves ahead, and every day we learn of self-organizing systems and theoretical strings and superstrings.

But these insights will not answer what John Horgan, staff writer for *Scientific American,* calls "The Question," which, he says, is, "Why is there something rather than nothing? In its effort to find 'The Answer' to 'The Question,' the universal mind may discover the ultimate limits of knowledge."[4]

All over the world and all through history, human beings have thought about Ultimate Reality. Some of them have proposed answers, but their answers are not all the same. Here we have another paradox: the people who do the most thinking finally come to understand that the Ultimate is beyond human understanding. *They understand that they cannot understand.* We are all agnostics.

Embracing the Mystery

If we are all really agnostics, then why should we even bother asking such questions? It's not as though we have a duty to ask them; it is simply that our human minds move in that direction because that is the way human minds work. We are a part of the universe that wants to know what the universe is all about. We want to know who we are and how we fit in.

That mysterious reality is a primary part of my life. I am committed to the *reality* of the mystery. Actually, the universe contains multitudes of lesser mysteries that we encounter all through our lives. Some of us refuse to think about them because we cannot explain them, but we need to be open to their reality. There are also many proximate questions that we probably can never fully answer. So I consider myself a faithful agnostic. It is not without pain, because no way of life is painless, but it is honest. It is also an exciting and strong way to live.

Every human being is equipped with a mind that reaches out through the stars and galaxies, back through time to the beginning of the universe and before, and ahead to the end of the universe and beyond. Every human mind asks, "Who am I and how do I fit in? What, if anything, does it mean, and what is life about? How should I live and why?" When we try to answer these questions, however, we find that we honestly don't know.

We Know We Don't Know

When I say that we know we don't know, that does not mean we don't know *anything*! Philosophers have argued about the relationship between what we think we know and the reality in which we live. What is the connection between whatever is out there and the thoughts and ideas that occur within our skulls? How do the vibrations in the air around us become our enjoyment of the music we hear? Sometimes a dream is so vivid that we react as if an external world were threatening us. The dream snake, a product of our inner mental processes, may be so frightening that we awaken in a sweat.

George Berkeley, the seventeenth-century Irish Bishop, held that God is real and our mental experiences are real. The external world is an illusion, emanating from God. Matter does not exist. When Samuel Johnson was asked by his biographer, James Boswell, how he would refute the argument of Berkeley, he kicked a large stone so forcefully that his foot rebounded from the contact. "I refute it thus!" Johnson said. But modern physicists tell us that the stone is a distribution of mathematical probabilities. We experience the solid hardness of stones, but actually the stone is mostly space. What our experiences tell us is, at best, only partially true.

Is it too flippant to say that what we can really know is that we don't know? At the level of existence in which we live, we can know some things. I know that as I write this I am sitting on a not-too-comfortable chair, pressing my fingers into keys that put electronic impulses into a computer, even though I really have no real idea how my computer works. However, we can know a number of things about the lives we live. My wife and I both know that we had a conversation last night. We both know—no, we and the couple who had dinner with us—that we talked about the church we all attend while we enjoyed coffee and dessert.

I know that I am happily married to Nancy, and I know that Meg and Jeremy live together. I almost said that I knew they were married. I think they are married, but I really don't know, and I know I don't care; that is their business, not mine. I know I hope that they are happy; I know that I think they are happy, because they seem to be happy. At least to me they seem to be happy. I think that Nancy thinks they are happy, but now I realize that we have never actually discussed it. Besides, she probably doesn't know any more about that than I do.

Countless times before now, I have thought a lot about what we know and how we know it. And now, without intending to, I have just reminded myself that we take many things for granted even in our everyday lives. We assume things about how the day will go, about when we will see one another, what time we will have dinner.

And yet we know that we don't know these things. Every time we say good-bye may be the last time we will speak to each other. Too many things happen on the streets, on the freeways. At any second, we may be inches from death. A driver coming the other way may be seized by a violent paroxysm of sneezing or startled by something she hears on her cell phone and unwittingly swerve across the median. Another driver may turn in front of someone who automatically cuts the wheel to avoid him, only to run into me. How often have I heard people sum up a close call with the phrase, "We just never know."

So I really do know that often we don't know. Reality is beyond our comprehension. The *Tao Te Ching* says, "The Tao that can be talked about is not the eternal Tao." Thomas Aquinas writes, "[God] exceeds . . . every form which our intellect attains." No human words or thoughts can really be the Ultimate Reality. Our words are like stubby little fingers pointing out to the distant galaxies, so we must not think that we have the universe in our hands! Even the closest reality is mysterious, and the Ultimate Reality completely eludes us. We know that we do not know.

Of course there are people who disagree with that idea. They *don't* know that they don't know, so they may therefore want everyone to accept what they see as truth: "We hold to an eternal principle, but you simply make personal decisions. If you admit that you don't know, then how can you take a stand? We at least have a basis for doing what we do. What basis do you have?"

When I say that I know that I don't know, I also mean that they don't know either. Nobody knows ultimate truth. Any declaration of ultimate knowledge is a form of idolatry, a manufactured deity, a human-made "ultimate." They have reached their position by making a personal decision. They accept what somebody tells them, or what they read somewhere, or maybe they form an idea of their own and decide that it is true. Then they commit their lives and well-being to their decision. If they encounter other people who believe some other authoritative source, they will simply maintain that the other source is in error.

Choice and Commitment

Once I find out that I face an important choice in commitments, I must decide which idea I own or which owns me. *My* values are those values that I affirm, that are part of my identity. I choose this and not that, because I think that this is better. If I felt the other were better, I would choose it. Our word *heretic* is derived from the Greek word meaning "to choose." A heretic is someone who chooses not to accept the majority view. It is equally true, however, that if someone chooses to follow the majority viewpoint, he or she is still choosing and is also therefore technically a heretic. Thus, Pascal could say that what is truth on one side of the Pyrenees is error on the other.

A similar situation is found with our word *protest*. We generally think that a protest is against some action or idea. A baseball player can protest an umpire's decision; citizens can protest a new law. Church members may protest developments in a church, as was the case with Martin Luther. However, if you protest something, you are actually testifying for something else, another idea. In Latin, the root meaning of *protest* means to witness for something. If you are for something, you are against its opposite.

We all have to make decisions; some are clear and others are confused, but we all have to make them, even though we don't know the ultimate answers. Part of being human is to decide what our values are. I may decide, let us say, that honesty and integrity are essential, that human relationships and human society can endure only if people can trust one another. A tyrant, of course, can run a society without the trust of the people, because he can force them to comply. But he also knows he has to be able to trust the people he chooses to assist him. If he cannot trust them, he can get no sleep. If he hires guards to protect him against his other guards, he fears that he will eventually hire one who cannot be trusted. Such unknowns are built into the universe, part of the way things are. So I am sure that honesty and integrity are fundamental values and that trust is a necessity of life.

Does the End Ever Justify the Means?

Nevertheless, there are exceptions. For example, if you were a citizen of a country ruled by a dictator, would it be right for you to pretend to be loyal in order to eliminate him? Can it be right to violate a fundamental ethical principle for the good of the whole society? Put another way, can treason under certain conditions be more honorable than cooperation? The Americans who signed the Declaration of Independence thought so.

You may well object, "You are saying that the end justifies the means. We have always been told that is wrong." My response must be, "Yes, and I agree that the idea is dangerous. But sometimes it can be wrong to follow a rule too rigidly. We should not forget that laws are made for people; people are not born in order to obey laws. Jesus pointed that out when he said, 'The Sabbath was made for humankind, not humanity for the Sabbath.'"

Look at a different situation. One of the basic rules of civilized society is that it is wrong to kill another human being. But suppose that you were to see a person with a knife sneaking up on a group of children. Suppose that you have the means and opportunity to stop him. If you had to choose, would it be better to kill him or to allow him to attack the children? Based on what I have said thus far, you cannot know for certain that he intends to attack the children. At best, it is hard to judge what another's motives might be. Perhaps you wait and watch for a while, to be as sure of the situation as you possibly can, but as you watch, it seems more obvious that he intends harm. Finally, you have to decide. Leave aside how you see your own personal courage. Look only at what you believe would be the right thing. Is it better to kill than to allow certain harm to others? Which is more important, the basic rule against killing or the lives of the children? I am not in favor of vigilante justice, but the point is that even our unchanging rules must change some of the time.

Dilemmas come with the human territory. A dilemma is a situation in which we don't know what to choose. Still, we have to make decisions. Usually they are not as extreme as in this imaginary confrontation with a knife murderer, but they could be. We have to live and act in this world even though we don't know all the answers. This principle applies not just to matters of life and death and morality and ethics. It also includes the need to act without all the required information when it comes to choosing a life partner or a career or deciding when to move to another job, another city. It's about how we decide to join a church, vote in an election, buy a house or car.

Knowing that we do not know does not mean we don't have to decide, but it can keep us from being arrogant about our knowledge, our virtue, or our own rightness. Knowing that other people have to make decisions under the same conditions, we can make necessary judgments without being judgmental.

Sometimes people break the rules in order to take advantage of others, and that is what is meant by criminal action. Other people break rules because they believe that a higher good will be served. For example, Martin Luther broke the rules of the Catholic Church because he believed that it had become corrupt and needed to be changed. When he was ordered to appear before a church council to retract what he had written, he obeyed the rule and appeared, but he refused to retract what he had said. "Here I stand," he concluded. "I can do no other, so help me God." His action changed the course of the world.

Rule breaking, however, is not to be undertaken casually. Sometimes people are punished, even killed, because of it. In the American civil rights movement, Rosa Parks, Martin Luther King, and many others risked imprisonment and death. It's not an accident that the early Christians who died for their faith were called *martyrs*. The Greek root word is the same as the word that means "witness." You bear witness to what you stand for, and that may mean that you have to pay a price. You never know.

Ignorance, Not Knowing, and the Gift of Reason

The phone rang just as Nancy and I were getting ready to eat our dinner.

"Darn telephone sales!" I muttered. I was sure it was somebody trying to sell us a trip to a time-share resort or maybe a new mortgage. But you never know, so I usually answer the phone even when we are not in the market to buy anything.

"Hello," I said, trying not to sound too annoyed.

"Hello, Joe?" came the response.

I recognized the voice. "Yeah!" I said. "How're you doing, Jeremy?"

"Fine," he said. "Is this an okay time to call?"

"Well, we are just about to eat. Can I call you back in a half hour or so?"

"Sorry about the timing!" he said with a little chuckle. "I knew it was dinnertime because we just had a call offering us a good rate on new aluminum siding! But this won't take long. Meg and I got to talking about the dinner we shared with you the other night. We really enjoyed that! But we thought of some ideas that we didn't talk about and we thought it might be fun to continue the conversation. How about brunch, maybe Saturday morning?"

"Sounds good," I said. "Let me check with Nancy."

I asked Nancy and found that it would fit her schedule; Jeremy and I confirmed the time. When I returned to the dinner table, Nancy said, "Well, that pretty well shows that you're right, doesn't it?"

"What do you mean?" I asked.

"That unexpected invitation to brunch. Just goes to show that you never know."

"Oh, yeah," I said. "Of course, lots of unexpected things happen in this world."

"It illustrates the point," she said. "We don't know what's going to happen in two or three days. We don't even know what will happen tomorrow or even later this evening. That little brunch invitation alters the shape of next Saturday for us, doesn't it? We didn't have any plans we had to change, but it means that whatever other things we might have done, we cannot do. And then, as we discuss these ideas, we might see how to change the way we do things in the church. We may all be different after we have brunch together this week. At the very least, our get-together will become a part of the total history of the universe. That means that the universe will be different than it would have been. That little difference would not exist if we hadn't gotten that invitation from Meg and Jeremy, and we would not have gotten the invitation if we had not had that conversation the other night when they were here for dinner. And we invited them for dinner because we just happened to meet them after the movie several weeks ago. You see what I mean?"

"Sure, you're right," I agreed. "You just reminded me that an important ingredient in how I want to live my life is to try to remember how all the little, apparently insignificant events change the course of human history. I sometimes get too involved in looking at the forest, and I forget that a forest exists only because there are thousands of trees of different kinds and sizes. No one tree is of great significance, yet every one counts in making the forest."

"Right," said Nancy. "And the forest would not be the same if any tree were not in it. It would still be a forest, but it would be different."

I agreed with her. "And to enlarge the idea, if we have brunch with them on Saturday, the totality of the universe will be different from what it would be if we do not have brunch. But for the most part, I doubt that the distant galaxies will be much affected by whether we do or don't."

"Oh, come on," she said. "You know what I mean. I have heard you say that the scent of a rose or the song of a hermit thrush is as real as a supernova, that it isn't just big things like stars and galaxies that are real, that stars and galaxies exist because an infinite number of small particles of energy engage in brief interactions, and all those multitudes of invisible and constantly changing patterns of energy play their brief parts. So if the scent of a rose exists, it is just as real as a galaxy, and a baby is just as real as an empire. And the little events in the lives of ordinary people are as real as the actions of the United Nations. Don't you say that?"

"Yes, I do say that," I agreed, "and I really mean it. I think that individual people are important and that we need to pay attention to them. I guess what I should say is that we all need to pay attention to each other and to ourselves. But sometimes I get impatient and disgusted at human beings in general. As you know very well, I am really not very fond of people in masses, though I do love lots of individual people. But even those masses of people are important; the history of the world is full of them. All the little decisions affect the world in very real ways. And to be honest, that sometimes scares me. History is being driven by too many drivers, and a lot of them are not paying attention to the road. That's dangerous."

"Yes, it's very dangerous, and you know it scares me, too," she said. She paused a little before she went on. "I think that careless-ness and ignorance will destroy the world. And that's why I worry when you say that what we know is that we don't know. If we don't know, we'll continue to be bad drivers and steer ourselves over the cliff."

I was taken aback by her comment; she knows that I am not pleased by ignorance. "Yeah, but . . ." I said, "I don't at all disagree with you. Lack of knowledge is dangerous. We need all the informed intelligence we can get."

"One of the problems is that so many of us 'know' things that are not so, and then we act on the basis of our mistaken ideas," said Nancy. "A lot of people are very sure that they know what is true, and many of them are eager to make the whole world conform to their knowledge, but what they really have is ignorance."

"Ignorance is not the same as knowing that we don't know. To be ignorant is to be unknowing without being aware that you don't know. To know that you don't know means that you are aware that you don't have the full truth. My point is that knowing you don't know the whole truth doesn't mean that you don't proceed; it should mean that you proceed with caution and a certain humility. Maybe the most dangerous thing is to be arrogant and ignorant at the same time; being sure that you are right but with no awareness of the blanks in your knowledge. That kind of not-knowing leads human beings to go full speed ahead without regard for unknown dangers."

"I was going to say that's the kind of thing that leads a teenage driver to go too fast and lose control of the car," Nancy said. "But maybe we shouldn't blame teenagers too much. They lack experience, so we can't expect them to know how much they don't know. But do you remember that review of the movie *Titanic*? It suggested that the movie and the ship were symbolic of our technological society, with its claims that it has the solutions to all problems and is accident-proof; it tends to discard cautionary ideas and shouts, 'Full speed ahead!' Maybe that awful catastrophe would not have happened if they had not been so sure they were unsinkable, if they had listened to the warnings about icebergs."

"Exactly so! *Exactly*," I said. "Even if you know you don't know, you can still go ahead. But the knowledge that you don't have full knowledge should keep you alert and make you more cautious. That might help you avoid the danger or make the damage less extensive. But anyhow, you have to make decisions, no matter how little or how much you may know."

"Yes, I see that," Nancy said. "But how do *you* know you are right when you say that the remedy for arrogance and ignorance is a more sophisticated kind of knowing? Couldn't that be wrong, too?"

"It could be. I surely don't claim to be infallible, but I don't have to be sure I am absolutely right when I see someone else making a dangerous mistake. Put another way, I don't have to know where the safe path is before I shout to the helmsman, 'Look out! There's a catastrophe ahead!'"

"In other words," she said, "you don't have to know everything in order to know something, and you must act as responsibly as you can on the basis of whatever it is that you *do* know."

"Yes," I agreed. Then I added, "But remember, you can still make mistakes. Even when you can be pretty sure of the truth, it is important to see that what you know is not *the* truth, so to speak, but a share—a portion—of truth. Absolute truth is larger than any of us *can* know. You cannot be utterly sure you are not making an error that can lead to later regrets or disagreements. In fact, disagreements are almost certain to come, because the situation is sure to change, and new understandings will change what needs to be said and done."

Nancy arose and started to clear the table. "I guess you can say that truth is like dirty dishes. You can get things cleaned up and carefully put away, but you know that it is not done once and for all. New messes emerge and it all has to be dealt with again."

"Right. So I'll help you get this clutter cleaned up now, but I don't guarantee that will be an answer for all time!"

"Final solutions are dangerous!" Nancy affirmed with a shudder. "Look at what Hitler did with that idea! And that's my final word about it—for tonight."

Reasonable Faith and Faith in Reason

I almost always enjoy conversations, whether they are serious or playful. I learn about the people I am talking to, but I also learn things about myself as I share my ideas. Sometimes it is only in the attempt to set them forth that my ideas actually take shape. Sharing them gives them life.

Sometimes I speak as if a given idea is a final product rather than a work in progress, and that makes it easy to give birth to a premature judgment. An aphorism is not a philosophy, it's just a catchy phrase. For example, my words about the importance of "knowing that you don't know" could seem to disparage knowledge and reason. Surely, encouraging anyone to act without information and thought is a recipe for blunder stew, which is neither tasty nor safe.

Reason is a quintessential part of being human. Out of human reason come all our constructions, both physical and mental: language, agriculture, architecture, science, social structures, religious affirmations, moral systems. Reason is the fundamental tool that humankind uses in the production of all other endeavors. However,

by "reason" I do not mean only problem-solving and deliberate efforts to think things through.

Paul Tillich points out that we use the word *reason* in two ways.
One denotes the scientific method, logical strictness, and technical
calculation. This aspect, which Tillich calls "technical reason," is
the problem-solving tool we use in the processes of recognizing and
controlling reality. It is generally thought that the goals of such control are not provided by technical reason itself, but by faith or
philosophy. In most periods of Western culture, however, *reason*
denotes the source of meaning, of structure, of norms and principles.
Tillich writes that this type of reason is the basis of human language,
freedom, and all creative efforts. Without reason we would lack art,
ethics, and community life.[5] Reason is the defining human quality.

Therefore, the quality of reason is essential for the development
of faith. Only a being who has reason can be concerned and can
distinguish preliminary concerns from ultimate ones. The very idea
of the transcendent depends on reason. Reason is the preliminary
requirement for the development of faith, and therefore the act of
faith is the way by which reason makes its ultimate commitment.[6]

Tillich affirms that human reason is, of course, finite. All the
cultural activities by which we perceive our world and by which we
shape it are finite. But reason is aware that its power is limited,
especially as it is related to the Infinite. Reason itself knows that
ultimately it does not know.

Obviously this is not a new discovery. Powerful thinkers through
the ages have grappled with related problems of what we know and
how we know it. Some contemporary physicists have concluded
uneasily that physics has moved itself into the realm of metaphysics
and has begun to deal with ultimate questions formerly thought to
belong to theology or philosophy. So much ferment serves as an in-
dicator that new developments will emerge, moving things in perhaps
unanticipated directions.

Philosopher Joseph Wood Krutch wrote that it would be a pity
if humanity should relapse into

> . . . the seemingly hapless situation of primitive man when he
> felt that almost everything was a separate mystery and that there-

fore almost anything might be true. But it is now really unnecessary to choose between saying 'We can understand nothing,' and 'What I cannot understand must be untrue.' There is a middle position which consists in saying that the human mind has established a genuine contact with reality but that there is not yet—and possibly never will be—a perfect correspondence between the categories of our understanding, between the concepts which we use in thinking and the universe itself.[7]

We can apply this principle in our attempts to make sense of our own lives and our relationship to the Ultimate. The Infinite Mystery is beyond its grasp and reason knows this. Yet reason cannot discard its own reality and its own structure. If things are said about the Infinite that are in total contradiction to the structure of human reason, then reason cannot embrace the contradictions and keep its integrity. If, for example, one is told that the Infinite is holy compassion, and also that the Infinite will condemn the majority of the creatures it has produced to suffer eternally because they cannot meet the infinite requirements, even the finite human mind can see that this is nonsense. Either the idea of holy compassion or the idea of eternal damnation is wrong.

It is the human capacity for reason that enables a person to form a faith, an ultimate commitment; this faith commitment undergirds the thoughts and actions of the finite human being. Faith is not the same as knowing something, for human knowledge knows it cannot encompass the Infinite Mystery. Nor is the commitment strictly a logical construct, for reason knows that its abilities cannot construct the infinite. But reason goes as far as it can and then bets on the nature of the Infinite Mystery. In a way, the person says to himself, "I don't *know* about this, but it makes sense to me and I shall live accordingly."

When Reason Reaches Beyond Itself

Thus we bet on the capacity of our reason, limited as it is, to make at least some sense of the Mystery. Is it hostile? Is it loving? Has it any qualities of what we would call personhood? Does it demand that we come up with the correct answer to the infinite questions, though we do not have infinite intelligence? Or does it know that we can go only as far as our finite reason will take us? Does the Infinite that produced us demand that we finite beings should be infinite in our reason; does it punish us for not knowing final answers to every big question? My faith, my commitment, tells me that makes no sense. I have to live by trusting that the Infinite can at least be depended on not to be subhuman in its ways with us, limited as we may be. Our limitations are very much a part of what we are.

My reason takes me only so far, and my faith tells me to use my reason as well as I can, for that is the way I (and other human beings) must live. Faith and reason are like the yin and yang qualities in the familiar Taoist symbol:

The two dynamic shapes in the circle are in constant interaction; just as one seems to be the largest and strongest, the other one begins to appear in conjunction with it. Each contains aspects of the other, and in their interaction they form one symbol. Or put another way, faith and reason are like two sides of the same coin: they seem as opposite as heads and tails, but they are totally inseparable. I have faith in my reason; I bet my life on that faith.

Is that reasonable? In truth, I have faith that it is.

Kite String and the
Web of Interdependence

W hy is it so hard for us to see the paradoxes that permeate our lives? The reality of paradoxes sometimes catches us by surprise; maybe that is because we constantly look at separate parts of reality and then draw inadequate conclusions.

As babies, we learn to discriminate among separate things around us: Mama . . . Daddy . . . kitty . . . doggie. We learn that kitty says "meow" and doggie says "bow-wow." We learn that what things *are* and what they *do* are different. But then we have to learn that people are different but alike; that animals—even doggie and kitty—are alike, and finally we know that somehow the whole series of things and actions is bound in a reality that holds them all. We see that we live in a universe, not a multiverse.

But what holds everything together? John Horgan, a senior writer on the staff of *Scientific American*, interviewed dozens of outstanding scientists, exploring their ideas as to whether or not science may finally come up with a "theory of everything." The answers of these eminent thinkers vary widely. Some expect that science will ultimately come up with all the answers. Others hold to the contrary. Horgan himself says that the most mysterious of all stars is our sun. Much as it is studied, nobody really knows why sunspots form or why their numbers grow and diminish over a period of about ten years. He says, "Our ability to describe the universe with simple, elegant models stems in large part from our lack of data, our ignorance." The more we can see the complex detail of the universe, the more difficult it is to find a simple theory of how it became that way. He comments that though students of history are well aware of this paradox, scientists may find it difficult to accept. [8]

Fritjof Capra observes:

> A careful analysis of the process of observation in atomic physics has shown that the subatomic particles have no meaning as isolated entities, but can only be understood as interconnections between the preparation of an experiment and the subsequent measurement. *It shows that we cannot decompose the world into independently existing smaller units.* As we penetrate farther into matter, *nature does not show us any isolated "basic building blocks," but rather appears as a complicated web of relations between various parts of the whole.* These relations always include the observer in an essential way.[9] [emphasis added]

The Universe Includes Everything

This idea of the complicated web of interrelationships applies not only to atomic physics, but also to life itself. The Taoist concept of yin and yang reminds us that opposing forces are constantly and dynamically ebbing and flowing; light and darkness give each other meaning, and the presence of either implies the reality of the other. So it is with male and female, active and quiet, wet and dry, good and evil, and positive and negative electrical charges. There is folly in the wisest person, and even a fool does some things right.

The Greek philosopher Heraclitus (about 500 BCE) held that the universe is never-ceasing change, but in our contemporary Western way of thinking, we assume endless progress toward what we consider to be better. We forget that events long ago and far away may produce effects in the world today; we also forget that effects will emerge in our own lives because of choices we ourselves made decades earlier. We forget that even in a river running swiftly down a valley, there are back-eddies and currents that run in the opposite direction to the main stream. So also do the currents of human events produce whirlpools and counterflows.

Despite its back-eddies and minor whirlpools, however, the river is one river. Conflicting flows in the universe do not turn the universe into a multiverse; it is One, and it contains all things. Do not imagine that the universe is dysfunctional; it simply is not as simple as we sometimes think.

The Interdependent Web Is Very Real

I emphasize that the following is a factual story.

On a summer afternoon in 1915, in Oakland, California, something happened that changed your life. You have never heard about it, but it changed not only your life, but the lives of hundreds of other people.

Two high-school girls went by train into Oakland to do some shopping. They came from a town so small that most of the streets did not even have names. The girls planned to catch a return train at 4:10 PM, but they were late and had to wait for the next one.

On that second train, the young, newly-hired brakeman was making one of his first runs. He went down the aisles, punching tickets. When he had finished, he returned to where the girls were seated and began a conversation. What is your name? Where do you live? Are you in school? One of the girls said, as they were pulling into the station in their home town, "See, that's my house . . . right over there by that big tree. That house with the green trim."

"Good," said the brakeman. "In a few days I'm going to come over to your house and ask your father if I may marry you. You are the girl who is going to be my wife."

And so it happened. He asked her father, and the father indicated that they needed to get acquainted first. The young man who came courting was the man who was to be my father a few years later, and the girl, of course, was to be my mother. If she had not missed that first train, she and the brakeman would never have met; if they had not met, they would not have married; if they had not married, I would not have been born; if I had not been born, I would not have written this book. And if I had not written this book, you would not be reading it now. You would be doing something else.

The Interdependence of Freedom and Commitment

We had known Sam and Julia for three years; they were members of a congregation I had served for that amount of time. Nancy and I knew them fairly well. They had called me for an appointment to discuss what they called "a minor problem." They started by telling how, some six or seven years ago, they had had a long tense spell when they could not make up their minds about marrying. That was no surprise to me; many people get nervous when they think of what it means to form a long-term legal partnership with another person, even someone whom they love and have been living with. Somehow, the legal ramifications may make people feel trapped and vulnerable. They know that they are voluntarily limiting their freedom, something most men and women properly regard as precious.

Now Sam and Julia faced another decision: whether to start a family. Sam was worried because he did not know what kind of father he would be. His own father had left his mother right after Sam was born. Sam's mother had raised him alone. On the other hand, Julia told him that if they put off the decision much longer, she would be too old. By postponing the decision, they were in a sense deciding not to have a baby. "Choosing not to choose now is really a choice not to do it at all," she said.

Sam hastened to say that this was not what he wanted; he wanted a reality check, but he didn't know if he could give up his freedom. Both Julia and Sam were willing to make commitments, and I saw them as taking such commitments seriously. I could see also that they were committed to freedom, and they wanted to work through the issue while they still had the time and freedom to do so. In that way, both Sam and Julia showed their real integrity, for freedom is the foundation of integrity.

Of course, all human freedom is limited and finite. For example, I do not have the freedom to have been born into an Eskimo family; Sam does not have the freedom to be Queen Elizabeth I, and Julia is not free to be King Henry VIII. Nevertheless, it has been argued that even a prisoner in a dungeon has a certain level of freedom, some decisions and choices that are still possible. That is why Richard Lovelace could write, "Stone walls do not a prison make, nor iron bars a cage." Wordsworth later modified that sentence to say, "Stone walls a prison make, but not a slave." That is to say, a prisoner is still free to *think* what his integrity directs, and he is free to respond to his captivity with stubborn determination or acquiescent passivity.

Obviously, we have no choice as to whether or not we shall die, but even in facing our own deaths, we have some choice. Do I rebel and resist the inevitable, or do I recognize that dying is as natural as living and accept that death is the price one must pay for life? (Someone has pointed out that statistics clearly show the only common factor that can be found among all persons who die is that all have been alive.)

But the purpose of this chapter is not to focus on ways of facing death, though I am persuaded that we Americans in general need to be more thoughtful about that whole topic. Instead, the purpose here is to focus on the meaning of human freedom, the process of living in an uncertain world, and the necessity of making choices without knowing where those choices will take us.

Kite Strings

Freedom and commitment form one inseparable and very complex package, much as do faith and reason. If you think that freedom is important, you make a commitment to freedom, a commitment that is valid only if it is freely made. (Actually no commitment can be forced, for a forced commitment is merely a surrender.)

In 1977, I was teaching a class of gifted eighth graders in a middle school in Albuquerque. I had assigned the students each to create some object that could be a kind of fetish, that is, a symbol of their clan of shared values, as they thought of how they would live their lives. These gifted and talented students produced paintings, models, carvings—many kinds of things to represent their values. Another part of the assignment was to make a brief oral presentation, explaining why this particular fetish was chosen.

Charley produced a fine kite, well constructed, handsomely decorated, and complete with a tail and a long string for flying it. "I chose a kite because I want to rise, to get above the crowd," he said. "I am ambitious to be outstanding. I decorated the kite so it would be as attractive as I could make it, because I value myself and don't want to be grubby or cheap. The tail gives it stability; I want to be a stable, dependable person. And I included the string, because a kite cannot fly without string. You might think that if you just released the kite into the wind it could fly farther and higher, but in fact, if it didn't have the string to hold it against the wind, it would simply blow along like a piece of trash."

The string that holds the kite down is what enables it to go up! It wasn't that I hadn't known this; it was just that I had not thought about it in that way until Charley pointed it out. That bright middle-school kid gave me an image that has been important to my own life. I have come to see that a life without commitment, like a kite without string, restricts the ability to rise and results in aimless drift.

We can see the same idea in the image of a boat on a river. Without sail or motor or at least a pair of oars, it is subject to the currents of water and wind. Without the power to go against the current, the boat drifts and the passengers drift with it. Freedom, therefore, demands the power to go against the prevailing currents. Being able to follow fads is not freedom; actually, it may be a form of slavish conformity. Neither is compulsive nonconformity to be seen as freedom, for the consistent nonconformist is not free to conform.

In other words, to be free does not mean to live without boundaries or restraints. A glutton might want to consume a tableful of rich foods, the alcoholic might want unlimited access to wine or gin, and a drug addict might crave an endless supply of cocaine. Nevertheless, that person is not free; that person is compelled to indulge a craving for something, and therefore continuously does what he might wish to avoid at the deepest or highest level of being.

Freedom to Do What You Do Not Want to Do

It would be better to say that freedom means the liberty to follow your innermost values. Sometimes that might mean that you will yourself to do what you actually don't want to do. Consider a woman who deeply loves her baby: though she does not want to, she gets up in the middle of the night to tend to the crying child. If she were restrained from getting up, she would not be free. If she is able to get up, she exercises her choice to do what she most deeply wants to do. The same would be true of a man who wishes he did not have to go to work, but is glad that he has a job. If he were unemployed, he would not have the freedom to go to work.

This exemplifies the difference between freedom *from* and freedom *for*. Freedom *from* is the desire of the adolescent for freedom *from* parental control. That is the basis for saying, "I want the freedom to do what I want." But it is an immature freedom, one that that has no purpose other than shaking off control. It has not considered the question of purpose and meaning and cannot make a commitment—not even to the self, much less to a relationship or cause.

A mature person who is forced to pay a penalty for supporting some endangered value still knows she has acted in freedom, though she may regret or resent the penalty. She values the freedom to have been *able to act* for the value she holds dear. If she had not been able to take her stand, she would have felt constrained and frustrated. She would regret the inability to support her values. She would not see herself as free.

Both Sam and Julia understand that if they limit their freedom by making commitments, those same commitments contribute to their being free, mature persons. Nevertheless, they may eventually come to see certain commitments as mistaken or premature. If that should happen, they will again have to decide what actions they must take to be free persons, like kites with string.

Let's consider two quite different examples. In the first example, a person (or two people) may decide that a previous commitment to their marriage is no longer valid. In good faith, they had made their commitment to live together and be of mutual support. But stresses may erode that commitment; the man may get more and more deeply involved in achieving material success so that the marital relationship deteriorates. In a real sense, he is no longer the person to whom the woman made her commitment. He has a new commitment, to amassing money and/or power. The isolated woman may feel the need to terminate her commitment to a relationship that has lost its meaning. Perhaps it is the woman who becomes somebody else; she may choose devotion to some ascetic religious movement or she may start to spend money wildly and get the couple into financial difficulties. While divorce and separation are always sad, for they indicate the death of hopes and dreams, sometimes that is the best choice a person has.

Of course, another possibility is that the distressed couple may agree to discuss the gone-wrongness of what they once shared. They may, by their willingness to talk and listen, be able to develop a relationship with new levels of understanding and commitment. In any case, an old commitment has deteriorated and has been replaced by a new one, a different one that honestly acknowledges the changes. Another instance is that of spiritual enlightenment or conversion. (To be enlightened is to see things in a new way, "in a new light." Conversion means to be changed; one can convert dollars to pesos or pounds, and one can be converted from materialism to a different value system.)

Commitment and Conversion

One of the best known instances of such change is St. Paul. When he was known as Saul, from the city of Tarsus, his commitment was to uproot the trouble-making splinter group of Jewish sectarians who had been followers of that upstart Jesus. Why did Saul of Tarsus commit to this action? These "Jesus people" publicly proclaimed that Jesus was the long-awaited Messiah, and that although he had been executed, he still lived and his followers had experienced his presence. This contributed to the ferment of competing ideas in Judea, which troubled the Jewish leadership and could have proved dangerous to all Jews if the Romans concluded that the movement threatened Roman power.

However, while he was traveling to Damascus to carry out his commitment to challenge the followers of the Jesus group, he was changed. He had a mystical experience, a vision of the living presence of the man whose followers he was oppressing. Paul was converted. He became convinced that his former commitment was mistaken; he was convinced that he had been fighting against truth, or, as he saw it, he had been fighting God. His new commitment changed his direction, and he now saw it as his duty to try to spread the message that he had formerly tried to strangle. The point is that nobody can guarantee that a commitment will never change, because *never* is a very long time! Even a commitment seen as a duty to God may sincerely be changed when the unexpected presents us with a new life direction.

But when people commit to bringing new life into the world, there is an additional dimension. Paul knew that God would survive without his help, but if Sam and Julia decide to have a child, that child cannot survive without their devoted attention and support. Children must be protected and taught until they reach adulthood, so freedom to produce children goes hand-in-hand with long-term responsibility.

If in the future, Sam's and Julia's relationship should become destructive to them or their child, they will need to face painful decisions. Their commitment to each other may end, but their commitment to their child must be absolute and nonnegotiable. One can be an ex-husband or an ex-wife, but one cannot be an ex-parent. However, the mere possibility that there might be a problem some day in the future does not mean that they should refrain from an honest commitment today.

What they can do with integrity is to say, "At this time, knowing what we know, seeing what we see, believing what we believe, this is our sincere and wholehearted commitment. We neither intend nor seek any change." No one can promise more than that; it is the best string a kite can have.

To have freedom, you must restrict your freedom. Life's paradoxes are signs of the complexity of the real universe. We cannot escape them. We must learn to live with them and in them.

A Small Platoon of Paradoxes

We conclude the first part of the book with a listing of some of the paradoxes we face. Their inescapable crosscurrents buffet our lives whether we are aware of them or not.

- *If you are trying too hard, it does no good to try harder not to try so hard.*

- *If you wish not to desire too much, wanting too much not to want so much will defeat your hopes.*

- *Facts must be true, but truth is not merely facts.*

- *One of the most important things to know is that we do not know.*

- *To be agnostic (not knowing) is not contrary to faith.*

- *Faith is not assenting to a set of beliefs; it is betting your life on your commitments.*

- *Knowledge, whether scientific or philosophical, ends in mystery.*

- *To be for something is also, at the same time, to be against something else.*

- *Sometimes breaking the rules is the truly moral or ethical behavior.*

- *Knowing that you do not know is not the same as ignorance.*

- *Even unimportant events are important.*

- *Though we know we don't know, we cannot choose not to choose.*

- *Faith and reason are mutually interdependent.*

- *Freedom and commitment are mutually interdependent.*

- *Choice is dependent on freedom; freedom depends on commitment; commitment limits our choices.*

- *Freedom is not freedom until it has purpose.*

- *Even deep commitments may legitimately change as the universe changes.*

The second part of this book is for all who seek ideas as they make their decisions about their spiritual lives. It is a way to include these paradoxical ideas in an overarching set of thoughts; in brief, it is theology for doubters.

Part Two

THEOLOGY *for* AGNOSTICS

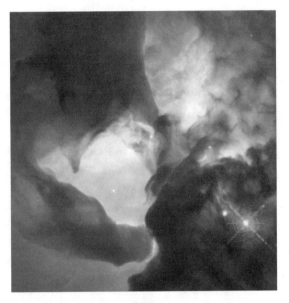

*My atheism . . . is true piety towards the universe and
denies only gods fashioned by men in their own image,
to be servants of their human interests.*

—George Santayana

A Preliminary Parable

Some mentally advanced atoms in one molecule of a white blood cell in a capillary in the interior of a human foot are thinking. They have devised ways to look out into the distant parts of their universe. They see collections of cells—galaxies containing millions of molecules and multiplied millions of atoms. The galaxies are far away, unimaginably far for the atoms. Their instruments tell them that their universe is growing and changing. They develop better instruments and scan the records left by previous atoms, and they realize that they are not as isolated as they thought they were. They are sure now that their universe has grown; there are distant clumps of cells with all the molecules that compose them, beyond the discerning abilities of their best instruments.

"Our universe is expanding!" they say. "We think it all started long ago with one clump of molecules and has expanded ever since!" (They call that idea "The Large Explosion.") How big their universe is they can only speculate. Some of the more imaginative atoms have suggested the possibility that there may even be other universes completely beyond their theories and knowledge.

The intelligent atoms there in that molecule in a cell belonging to a human immune system debate the issue: "Is there any meaning in this universe beyond our own intelligence? Can there be a purpose for all this dynamic arrangement and interaction of distant molecules?" Some of them assert that there is not, for they cannot discover it anywhere, nor can they imagine what such a purpose would be. Others agree that they cannot discern such a purpose, but they feel that somehow, such complexity as they can see is not simply meaningless. Surely, these vast electromagnetic and chemical interactions are not just accidents!

Meanwhile, the body in which the thoughtful atoms carry on their debate belongs to a student who is working on a term paper. The topic is, "What is the meaning of human life?"

Personal Faith in a
God That Does Not Exist

The student was speaking earnestly to a professor of theology, one of the visiting lecturers at a university forum on "Religion, Ethics, and Modern Society."

"I question the idea of this whole forum," the student said. "Honestly, I don't believe in God."

"I see," said the visiting professor. "What kind of god do you not believe in?"

"I don't believe in a God who in a short time suddenly created the universe, or who changes the course of events in answer to prayer, or who keeps track of our daily behavior so we can be rewarded or punished. None of that stuff."

"Good!" said the lecturer. "Neither do I. So, what is your question?"

No Such Thing As an Unbeliever

In Greek, the word *theos* means "God," and *logos* means "word, discourse, or study." The derived English word *theology* means "a discourse or an organization of ideas about God." How can there be a theology for unbelievers, for those who assert that they do not believe in God and see no need for the idea of the divine?

Strictly speaking, there are no unbelievers; everybody believes something. For example, even an ardent atheist who asserts that he does not believe that there is a God is at the same time asserting that he believes that there is no God. The matter cannot be proved either way. So essentially, when we call someone an unbeliever, we are really saying that he believes that most of what is said about the Ultimate is wrong or irrelevant. If he does not believe in God as a symbol for the Ultimate Reality, he believes in something—the laws of physics, the universe as a whole, perhaps nature. He believes that something is ultimate, but his belief is different from that of the avowedly religious person.

It is quite possible to be a human being without giving much thought to Ultimate Reality. Like dogs, wart hogs, zebras, catfish, and all other animate beings, human beings have physical needs that must be met if the organism is to survive—food, water, shelter, and some way to reproduce. Obviously, these needs can be met without recourse to philosophical or religious ideas, but in general, we regard such a basically physical level of living as minimal for the kind of being we call "human." Even by age two, little children point with delight at the moon or the flowers and are deeply aware of relationships with people around them.

However, it is possible for a person to claim that she has no interest beyond getting enough to eat, having adequate shelter, and perhaps deriving some pleasure in other aspects of human life such as sexuality or music or friendship. She can enjoy music or the sounds of the natural world and can appreciate them without thinking of those human dimensions that are beyond sheer physical existence. Such pleasures do not demand any idea of God or the transcendent in order to be enjoyed. Once we become aware that we are enjoying something, however, our very awareness takes us beyond the raw experience. We are already living in two dimensions: the dimension of enjoying something and that of knowing that we enjoy it. The human mind inevitably takes us beyond sheer existence.

When I explain these concepts in one of my classes, Janice, a student, raises a question. "You said that when we are enjoying something and we become aware that we are enjoying it, we are doing two things at the same time—we are doing something and we are *thinking about* what we are doing. Am I right?"

"Yes, that is what I meant," I respond.

Janice continues, "I suppose that really does make humans different from other creatures. If a cow is eating grass, it is probably not saying to itself, 'Wow! This is really delicious grass.' It just eats the grass and chews and swallows, then steps forward for another bite without considering what it is doing. It sort of gets the raw experience without the analysis. But are we humans any better because we can think about what we are doing? Maybe the cow has a more direct experience of eating than we do, because we get self-conscious about things. That is not always good, is it?"

"No, it's not," I reply. "But first, I am not saying that it is necessarily always better to know or label your experience. I'm just saying that is the way human beings are. To be human means to know what you are doing, and to know that you know. We feel hungry and we know that what we feel is called 'hunger.' I doubt that cattle have that self-awareness—they just eat as they need and as they can. There is evidence that some of the higher primates have a degree of self-awareness, but it is highly doubtful that they can ask themselves what they know and how they know it.

"But sometimes our mental processes can make our lives a little unreal. We may think about being angry but not really experience the anger. We may eat but not really experience the taste. Maybe sex is so important to us humans because when we are involved in sex, we are not usually thinking about it in some abstract way. In fact, unless we can experience it directly, we miss the intensity and ecstasy. That's why there are those jokes about someone remarking during sex, 'I think we had better get the hall repainted,' or 'I wonder what is on TV now?' Sometimes our ability to think about one thing while we are doing something else dilutes our experience.

"However, that ability allows us to have memories, to stand in awe of sunsets, to enjoy theatrical performances. It enables us to ask questions about what is right and wrong, what is good, and why things are what they are. It's the foundation for professions such as law, science, and religion. It's also involved in all kinds of planning. It may have drawbacks, but it also has blessings and benefits. The ability to think about things takes us into the realm beyond raw experience. People do not live by their senses alone, but also by ideas and thoughts and imagination, by wishes and hopes. That is part of what Jesus meant when he said, 'A person does not live by bread alone.'"

"Well, of course," interjects Stan, another member of the class. "That's also why we can enjoy reading, isn't it? Because we look at the raw materials—the little marks that we call letters—and our minds form those little shapes into words, and then thoughts and ideas form in our minds and produce new thoughts. Sometimes I find myself reading and realize that my eyes are just moving along while my mind is off somewhere else, and I don't have any idea what the book says!"

Stan's point is valid: reading is indeed a complicated series of actions, but we seldom think about it while we are doing it. We put all of that out of our minds because thinking about the process of reading keeps us from doing the actual act of reading.

Some philosophers and scientists deliberately exclude any idea of God from their work. They do this for various reasons, depending on their individual backgrounds and purposes. Scientists in general properly exclude God from their theories (but not necessarily from their personal lives) because it is very poor science to explain a process by saying, "And then God makes it go," or "God balances the equations." Science is concerned with understanding the processes by which the universe operates at the infinitely large, the infinitely small, and in the finite middle. We do not find God in theories or in the processes that theories seek to explain. As Paul Tillich reminds us, "A God about whose existence you can argue is a thing beside others in the universe of existing things."[10] God is no thing, but that is not to say that God is nothing.

Stan sits up straight and interrupts with another question. "Hey, wait," he says. "Does that mean that God does not exist?"

"That's what Tillich says," I agree. "God does not exist."

"Well, how can you believe in anything that doesn't exist? That's like believing in dragons or unicorns or Godzilla, isn't it?"

"Not quite," I reply. "Tillich means that no matter how much you sort out the things in the universe, God is not among them. God is not a thing or an object, the existence of which can be proved or not."

"That is hard for me to get," Stan says. "Does that mean that God is just a product of the human mind? And if so, what is the difference between an idea of God and an idea of Godzilla?"

"Important question, Stan!" I respond. "There are probably a lot of levels to any answer to that question, but let me try two of them. First, our ideas of God are all products of the human mind. Any idea of God is not God; it is something our minds construct. Our minds also construct ideas of the universe, but they are not the same, and our ideas can be very wrong. There have been many mistaken ideas about the universe.

"So, sure. Any idea of God is a human creation, and we should not confuse it with Ultimate Reality. But unlike the idea of a totally fictional Godzilla, our ideas of God are attempts to interpret reality in its ultimate dimension.

"The main part of Tillich's thought is that God is not an existing thing or process. He speaks of God as 'The Ground of Being' or 'The Power to Be.' Tillich asks us to think about what existence means. What enables stars or galaxies or people or sharks to exist? I heard Tillich say one time in a lecture that he was walking in Central Park with his little daughter, and she asked him, 'Papa, why is that tree not *not*?' The real question is, 'Why is there anything instead of nothing?'"

I continue speaking to the class. "Remember that we really need to use metaphors or similes when we speak of God. These are figures of speech in which we compare two very different things, allowing one of them to give us an idea about the nature of the other. But they cannot be taken literally. For example, when the poet says, 'My love is like a red, red rose,' he doesn't mean that his beloved has thorns and leaves; he is saying that she is sweet, beautiful, and marvelous. So we say, 'God is like a father,' or 'God is king.' God is not literally either father or king."

The Light Behind the Action

If we try to set forth in a metaphor this idea about God not existing, I think it could go something like this. Suppose you imagine a motion picture: the scenery and the action are projected onto the screen. Now you might ask, how can these pictures move that way? When I say that light allows it to happen, you could say, "But I don't see the light—I just see the characters acting and talking!" The answer is that the light enables all the action to take place, all the characters to move, all the scenery to exist. The light is not in the action or in the scenery, and it is not part of them. It sustains them, it gives them the power to do what they do.

That is only an analogy or a metaphor, and it can't be stretched too far, but it gives an idea of how God can enable the process without being part of it. Another analogy might be that you will never capture the river while you are catching fish, frogs, and turtles because the net that catches the things in the water cannot catch the water that enables them to live. These analogies are not literally true, but you get the idea of what Tillich is saying. God does not exist; God empowers existence.

In any case, a person who excludes any contemplation of Ultimate Reality from her thoughts is clearly excluding ideas that are important to most human beings. Wherever we find people, we find beings who ponder and wonder about themselves, each other, the world they live in, and the universe of which they are a part. How is it that everything—that anything—came to be? Does existence have any meaning? Do we need something other than sheer biology to understand it? Psychology, which is a mixture of biology plus something else, tries to understand how the human mind works, but it does not include the meaning of being human nor the idea of the ground of being. These are essentially theological questions.

Such questions do not have factual answers, but that does not mean that they do not have any answers. Both questions and answers deal with what therapist James Hillman calls "the invisibles" that strongly affect human living.

> Usual life, too, is backed by invisibles, those abstractions of high energy physics that compose all the visible, palpable, and durable stuff we bump into; the invisibles of theology we kneel to; the invisible ideals that take us to war and death; the invisible diagnostic concepts that explain our marriages, our motives, and our madnesses. And what about time; has anyone seen it lately?[11]

We must avoid the simplistic idea that things that are invisible to or unmeasurable by science are nonreal. Electrons are invisible, yet science has evidence of their existence. On the macro level, black holes are invisible, yet astrophysicists can infer their existence by their effects on other stellar bodies.

But we must also remember that our lives are filled with a vast number of invisible but real qualities that have no measurable dimension under any magnification, but which guide us in our living. Ideas are invisible, but they have real and discernible effects. The idea of democracy is a strong human motivator; so are the ideas of freedom and power. Whole nations are moved into action by these invisible ideas. Individually, we are sent into action by ambition, love, envy, compassion, and loyalty. Often these invisible realities change our lives and the lives of people all around us; often they affect us without our thinking about them.

And that brings us to the relevance of theology for the skeptic or unbeliever. By "unbeliever" I am not speaking of one who seriously has thought and has come to believe, considering the best available evidence, that any concept of God is useless. I am not speaking of one who leaves God out of his theory because he is trying to see how the universe works on a mechanical level. I am speaking of and to the person who has not even tried to think of the invisibles because they are just too overwhelming.

The student in the anecdote at the beginning of this chapter thinks that she has no use for theology because she cannot accept the idea of a God who changes the course of events in response to prayer. She discards the concept of God as an infinite special prosecutor with unlimited time and power to investigate and condemn everyone in the universe who does not behave (or even think) in a certain ultrahuman manner. That student does well to set aside such an idea of Ultimate Reality, but rather than stop thinking altogether, she needs to think in different ways.

The important question is not, "Do you accept a certain stereotypical view of the nature of God?" but rather, "How do you conceive the nature of Ultimate Reality? What *does* make sense to you?" The student in the preceding paragraph has discarded a too-small image of God that she cannot believe in. She can say what she does not hold to, but she has no way of saying anything positive or affirmative.

Now let us imagine a student who is the opposite of the one in our opening anecdote. This student says to the theologian, "I have a question. How can you call yourself a theologian when you do not believe in a Creator who made the universe out of nothing nor that the laws of the Bible are divinely inspired and ordained forever?"

The theologian might answer, "I value the Bible, but the writers of those books never thought of electronic communications, or rockets, or telescopes for viewing the universe from orbits outside the earth, or atomic weapons that could wipe out all life. The idea of a king was the best way they had to think of God. Most of us live in democratic societies now, and we have to ask ourselves, 'How can we best think about God and the universe in ways that will make sense *to us?*' I am not suggesting that we should think of God as President or Prime Minister, but the metaphor of God as a powerful king doesn't make as much sense to us now. In fact, absolute rulers—such as dictators, who are most like the kings of ancient times—represent the raw use of power to keep their subjects under control. Is that an appealing concept of God? If not, then what makes better sense?"

The theologian could continue, "The writers of the biblical books told people to go forth and multiply, but they could not have foreseen the horrors of overpopulation. They couldn't have conceived of the prolongation of human life through artificial devices and organ transplantation. They did not have to face the reality of millions of people living so long that their own lives become a burden to them.

"The writers of those books thought deeply about God, but they knew that they did not know everything and that ultimately, God was a mystery. We moderns also know that we do not know ultimate truth, yet we know some things that we cannot ignore. We must try to think of the Ultimate in our time even as they tried to in their time. We honor them, not by freezing their ideas, but by following their example and finding ideas that make sense to our own time and to our own integrity. Otherwise, we betray their vision."

Furthermore, our imaginary theologian would remind a questioner that human beings were thinking about the Ultimate for perhaps hundreds of millennia prior to recorded Scripture. Are all those millions to be condemned because they lived before the Bible was written? Let us keep in mind also that not one of those writers whose work came to be included in the Bible had any concept that he was writing for that purpose. Six centuries would pass from the writing of the earliest parts of the Bible until the resulting books came to be regarded as "Scripture."

Additionally, multiplied millions of people in other lands have faced the sublime Mystery, and in their differing ways, have also tried to understand our relationship to that which is behind or beneath or beyond the visible world. Can we ignore their combined wisdom and vision?

Actually, these words—*behind, beneath, beyond*—are simply spatial metaphors to help us think about more than the physical world. The world is smaller, the universe is bigger, and time is longer than people formerly thought. We should consider these things as we try to think responsibly and freely about our own personal theologies.

I speak of "personal theologies," for I neither strive for nor believe in the possibility of one all-embracing system of theology, covering all aspects of belief and applying to all human beings. Such a system is not really feasible. Thomas Aquinas, the great Catholic theologian, wrote his *Summa Theologiae* in the thirteenth century in an effort to put together an inclusive compendium of theology. Similarly, John Calvin's *Institutes of the Christian Religion* (sixteenth century) was intended as a summation of a cohesive system of theology. However, both these great works came to be surrounded by many interpreters and modifiers, even before the coming of the rapid changes produced by the scientific revolution.

Today, honest doubters interpret the faith stances of their respective churches according to their own personal integrity. They will say, "I am a loyal Catholic (or Lutheran, or Baptist, or whatever), but I really don't believe such and such an idea . . ." Even in groups with notably homogeneous viewpoints, there are multitudes of people who take quiet and private exception to the prevailing ideas of their companions. Neither the rapid changes in worldview nor the pervasive commitment of individuals to their own sense of truth will support the idea of a single systematic theology for all.

Mahatma Gandhi was committed to the idea that all religions are true, but all are imperfect, and we are not to overlook the imperfections. Rather, we should see the values they uphold even if their adherents do not achieve them. Gandhi wrote:

> Why should there be so many different faiths? The Soul is one, but the bodies which She animates are many. We cannot reduce the number of bodies; yet we recognize the unity of the Soul. Even as a tree has a single trunk, but many branches and leaves, so is there one true and perfect Religion, but it becomes many as it passes through the human medium. The one Religion is beyond all speech. Imperfect [people] put it into such languages as they can command, and their words are interpreted by other [persons] equally imperfect. Whose interpretation is to be held to be the right one? Everybody is right from his own standpoint, but it is not impossible that everybody is wrong.[12]

It is important for an individual to know what he values, what she bets her life on. For simple personal integrity, a human being tries to fill in some of the blank spaces in the mystery. I look at the constantly shifting universe around me to put together some relevant ideas to give myself some ground on which to stand. I speak not simply of the physical universe, but of the universe of human understanding and perception. My understanding of what values are most important in life, of what things benefit or hurt the world, of what attitudes and actions enable people to live together, guide my decisions and my ways of being a member of human society.

But at the same time, it is important that I not assume arrogantly that accepting my theology is essential to my neighbor. He has his own theology; she bets her life on her own values. Their answers do not have to be my answer, though if we are to live in the same society, we must agree to respect each other's integrity.

That gives me one important part of my personal faith system: *to be reality-based, respect for other people's search for truth must be a central part of it.* My theology is important to the way I live, but I do not insist that everyone follow the same set of ideas. If my theology is to be rooted in reality, it must not break the bonds that enable people to live together. In other words, if my theology insists that only I and those who agree with me have the truth and that all others are inferior in some way, that is a very good sign that my theology is too narrow. It breaks the threads on the human tapestry and damages the world. It is difficult to reconcile such damage with even an idea of principles by which the human world can live in peace and harmony. My understanding of reality must contain in its center the principle that Ultimate Reality is larger than any single idea of it, including my own.

However, one does not have to agree with people who hold differing views; one simply must respect their right and freedom to explore for meaning after their own integrity. But the fact that I hold a minority opinion does not mean that I am wrong. It is all right to hold to a differing perspective on reality if you do not use it to coerce your neighbors, and it is also right for you not to submit to their coercion.

The agnostic or unbeliever is already convinced that no human system can know all the possibilities of truth and that no person or group has sole possession of it; indeed, such conviction may be a major reason for the lack of belief that characterizes the unbeliever's life.

So here is where we are:

- It is part of being human to think of meanings and Ultimate Reality.

- Invisibles are a very powerful part of human life.

- We must think of God in metaphors and ideas that make sense to us in our time and in our world.

- We must think in terms that will respect and honor the people who are outside our culture.

- Truth is not decided by majority vote.

- We are not trying to achieve a universal understanding of one truth.

From the beginning, it is important to know that any theology that may emerge from our thoughts cannot be final. It should be, though, at least a beginning.

Thinking About the Unthinkable

N ancy was out for the day, and I had gone to get some groceries and other household supplies from the supermarket.
As I passed the little coffee shop next to the grocery store, I
decided to go in for an afternoon latté. When I entered, I saw Mark,
a member of one of my classes. He was looking at the sports page
from the morning paper as he sipped his coffee. I went over to his
table. "Hi, Mark! How's it going?"

He looked up and grinned. "Hi, Joe! I'm just killing time waiting for Janice. She'll be here in a few minutes, and then we are going
out to see some friends who invited us for a picnic at their place in
the mountains. Come on and join me." I went to the counter and got
a latté, then sat across the small table from Mark.

"I'm glad you happened to come in," he said. "I was talking this
morning with one of my friends down at the office about religion.
He is a humanist, and he regards all religion as superstition—simply
a product of the human mind. He says that if I want to be really
honest, I will just screen out all that speculation and admit that all
the values that count are the product of the human mind. He says
that human beings created God. What he said kind of made sense,
and it raised a lot of questions. Is he right?"

"Pretty much," I said. "I think there is strong evidence for that.
The religious systems all over the world came out of human minds,
were put together by human thinkers, and are interpreted by human
beings. All of them evolved through time. They all have moved in
different directions and have developed different branches and in-

terpretations. Human beings created ideas of gods or God in an attempt to make sense of themselves and their world. And it was human beings who set forth the rules that shaped their societies and the way people related to each other. Value systems and religions and philosophies are products of human beings. They did not get to earth by heavenly chariots."

I sipped some latté as Mark said, "Then why is it not more honest just to admit that and simply discard all those human religious systems?"

"Mark, what your friend forgets is that the philosophy he follows, which he says is the only honest way, is also a human system. It is not infallible or perfect; it is the product of people who seriously want to make sense of the universe and life and death, and so it must be respected.

"But that outlook can be self-centered when it insists that there is no meaning in the universe except what human beings provide," I said. "It overlooks the vast mysteries that are beyond human understanding. How can we claim to know the final answers, that we have the highest knowledge? Upon what information do we base that assertion? How do we know that there is no intelligence except human intelligence?"

I continued, "Your friend does not propose an alternative that prefers facts to faith; he offers simply a different kind of faith, which is also the product of the human mind. It is a valid approach, but sometimes it forgets what it really is, namely, another human faith system. Scientific humanists sometimes sound as if they have a special kind of knowledge and that every other stance is superstition."

I knew I was speaking with a certain passion, for even as I oppose the narrow certainty of the religious fundamentalist, I resist the narrow reductionism of the humanistic fundamentalist. Fundamentalism in any form is tinged with a narrow-minded sense of superiority to all the "unenlightened" who pursue a different way.

"But, Joe," said Mark, "if you want to avoid superstition and arrogance, what kind of Ultimate Reality can you bet your life on? What conviction can you hold to without being narrow-minded or arrogant? I've read somewhere that even in the Bible, God is different in the Old Testament and in the New Testament. If even the

Bible has differing ideas of God, what makes us think that we can straighten it out?"

"Yes," I said. "There are not only differences in the perception of God in the two testaments, but even in the Hebrew Scriptures there are differing ideas of God. After all, the Hebrew Bible was written over a span of nearly ten centuries, and people lived in differing conditions during that time. Of course their ideas changed and grew.

"But please keep in mind that I don't have any idea of straightening anything out. I have tried to emphasize that point all through our classes together. I simply think that we must face the ultimate mystery of the universe and make the best sense of it we can.

"One of the first things we have to face honestly is that there are mysteries both unexplained and unexplainable. In fact, we should celebrate the mystery! Which means that we won't try to capture God in a formula, but that we will open our minds and hearts to live creatively in the mystery, knowing that we don't know the answers."

"And here comes Janice," Mark said. He waved to her and she came over to the table. Janice greeted me warmly, and then she and Mark walked out arm-in-arm. I went on and got my groceries before I headed for home, wondering all the while how I could write about God.

Speaking of the Unspeakable

I remember the old story of a little boy who was very busy with his crayons, putting many shapes and colors on a piece of paper. "What are you drawing, dear?" his mother asked. He said, "I am drawing a picture of God."

"You can't draw God," said his mother. "Nobody knows what God looks like."

"That's why I'm drawing the picture," said the boy. "They will now!"

That youngster, of course, was a little ingenuous, and I feel somewhat abashed as I try to put down some ideas about God, the ultimate mystery. How do I dare to speak of that about which nothing can be spoken? My only excuse is that I see my words as pointers toward the sublime. I have found small visions of it when I look in that direction. Maybe sharing those glimpses will help you too.

In the Taoist classic *Tao Te Ching* (*The Book of the Way and Its Power*), the opening words are, "The Tao (way) that can be told is not the Tao. The name that can be named is not the sacred name." The book is often attributed to the legendary philosopher Lao Tsu, who was supposed to have lived in about the sixth century before the Common Era. It is one of the most sacred books in Taoism. Thus, this ancient book, speaking of *tao*—"the way things are"— treats it as a mystery that cannot even be spoken of accurately. In other words, what we try to say about the ultimate way is beyond our speech, beyond our thought.

The Christian tradition has its own echoes of this idea. In the fifth century, St. Augustine wrote, "We conceive God, if we can . . . without location, being wholly everywhere without a position, eternal, without time . . . If you understand God, it is not God you understand." In the thirteenth century, Meister Eckhart observed, "Whoever perceives something in God and attaches thereby some name to him, that is not God. God is ineffable." Similarly, the great Catholic theologian Thomas Aquinas said, "[The Divinity] exceeds by its immensity every form which our mind attains . . . The highest understanding we can have of God in this life is that we realize that God is beyond everything that we might think of him."

The very knowledge that the mystery always eludes us can give us a deep appreciation of its awesome character. Albert Einstein said that the most wonderful thing we can experience is the truly mysterious, and he reminds us: "The important thing is not to stop questioning; curiosity has its own reason for existing. One cannot help but be in awe when contemplating the mysteries of eternity, of life, of the marvelous structure of reality. It is enough if one tries merely to comprehend a little of this mystery every day. The important thing is not to stop questioning; never lose a holy curiosity."[13]

So we are about to attempt what great theologians and philosophers tell us is impossible, namely, to speak in some meaningful way of the Ultimate Reality that many people name God. We make no effort to define that which is beyond all definition, for to define is to draw a boundary around something. Nevertheless, knowing that our efforts are at best limited, we shall look at a few ideas that can be helpful as we, like Einstein, try "to comprehend a little of this mystery every day, and . . . never lose a holy curiosity."

We have already affirmed that the Ultimate is a mystery that our minds cannot penetrate. Our awareness and acceptance of the idea that the mystery is impenetrable gives us an understanding that is worth more than comprehension. But even so, there are some things that might help us to understand how we can think about it. We remind ourselves that the purpose of our theologizing is simply to find ideas and values that, in our own lives, will help us approach our own faith stance, our own ultimate commitment.

One of the fundamental questions is whether the ground of being is personal in some sense. The Bible says that we were made in the "image of God." Is there any way that can be true? In other words, does the Ultimate have any qualities on which human beings are patterned in some way? Does "It" for example, know that it has being?

The answer is that we don't know. But somehow, the universe has produced us, and we know that we exist. We are a part of the universe that asks, "What are we? What is this universe of which we are a part?" Through us, the universe looks at itself and knows that it has being. But outside our human experience, does the universe in any other way know that it exists? We do not know whether the mystery that produced the universe knows or not. However, it seems colossally arrogant to assume that out of all the vast cosmos, only we organic specks on a small planet circling a medium-size star in one of billions of galaxies have such knowing.

Is the mystery that produced life less intelligent than the human creatures that emerged on this small planet? Again, we don't know, but my faith, my bet, my reason is that the mystery is not less intelligent than we are, even though how the mystery knows and what it knows are beyond my comprehension. Instead of thinking of the divine as personal (like us), it is probably better to think of it as transpersonal. C. S. Lewis calls one of his books *Beyond Personality*, and that is a good way of suggesting that God is not subhuman, not beneath personality.

The developments of modern physical science offer another perspective. I do not pretend to understand this astonishing unfolding of the atomic and subatomic universe. To compensate for my own lack of knowledge, I will share some quotations from a number of knowledgeable people who have written about modern physics. (In my lack of understanding, I find myself in good company. Niels Bohr, one of the early pioneers in the realm of the quantum, is often quoted as having said that anyone who is not shocked by quantum theory has not understood it. Physicist and astronomer Edward Harrison also notes that Bohr said, "When it comes to atoms, the language that must be used is the language of poetry.")

Therefore, I freely share the poetic visions of Harrison's fine book, *Masks of the Universe*. His words abound in poetic images as he discusses the new view of atoms and particles:

Once it was the custom to imagine the atom as a miniature solar system with electrons encircling the nucleus like planets orbiting a sun. This idea still exists in popular literature. But electrons do not move in clear-cut orbits like revolving celestial bodies. They dance, and the atom is a ballroom. The electrons perform stately waltzes, weave curvaceous tangos, jitter in spasmodic quicksteps, and rock to frenetic rhythms. They are waves dancing to a choreography composed differently for each kind of atom.[14]

Harrison continues his analogy of energy particles as waves:

The electron waves spreading out and interweaving wherever possible account for the structure of atoms. They lace together arrays of atoms into molecular tapestries and create the rich and varied patterns of our world of plants and flowerpots.

How can a tiny electron behave like a widespread wave? We must face the fact, as much as any we know, that all subatomic particles, not only electrons, have a remarkable dual nature. At one moment a particle is like ripples on a pond, and at the next moment like a cherrystone in the palm of the hand . . . its dual nature is as perplexing as the duality of mind and matter. The strange quantum world contains nothing of our world of commonplace experience, and we must not try to comprehend things in the vulgar fashion.[15]

The word *vulgar* is here used in its original sense of "common, ordinary, everyday." (Thus the first translation of the Bible into Latin was called the *Vulgate* because Latin was the everyday language.) Harrison simply means that we cannot use common sense and ordinary ways of seeing to understand the strange world of quantum physics. British scientist J. B. S. Haldane said, "The universe is not only stranger than we imagine, it is stranger than we *can* imagine."

Of course, we who are uninitiated ask, "How do those people know all this? How can scientists know what the invisible universe is like?" I have already acknowledged that I do not comprehend how mathematicians and physicists reach their conclusions. Their own accounts show that they use intuition and logic, and they design experiments. They also use very advanced mathematics to describe the relationships between the various forces and energies and particles. Their equations go on at great length; the experiments and the mathematics reinforce each other, and their work is rigorously critiqued by their peers. From time to time they have to modify their ideas. Meanwhile, as a nonmathematician and nonscientist, I am glad to take their ideas on faith!

Gerhard Staghun quotes Werner Heisenberg, another scientist who helped lay the foundation for the structure of quantum mechanics, as follows:

All the elementary particles can, at sufficiently high speeds, be transmuted into other particles, or they can simply be created from kinetic energy and can be annihilated into energy, for instance, into radiation. Therefore, we have final proof of the unity of matter. All elementary particles are made of the same substance, which we may call energy or universal matter.[16]

A more recent interpreter of the new physics is Fritjof Capra, who has done research in high-energy physics at several European and American universities. In *The Tao of Physics*, he writes:

[Quantum theory] has abolished the notion of fundamentally separated objects, has introduced the concept of the participator to replace that of the observer, and may even find it necessary to include the human consciousness in its definition of the world. It has come to see the universe as an interconnected web of physical and mental relations whose parts are defined only through their connections to the whole.[17]

Later in the same book, Capra writes:

These dynamic patterns or "energy bundles" form the stable nuclear, atomic, and molecular structures which build up matter and give it its macroscopic solid aspect, thus making us believe that it is made of some material substance. At the macroscopic level, this notion of substance is a useful approximation, but at the atomic level it no longer makes sense. Atoms consist of particles and those particles are not made of any material stuff. When we observe them we never see any substance; what we observe are dynamic patterns continually changing into one another—a continuous dance of energy.[18]

These ideas cast one more uncertain dimension into an old bit of word play:

"What is mind?"

"No matter."

"What is matter?"

"Never mind."

"But what is mind?"

"It is immaterial."

In a sense, quantum physics says to us that the material universe itself is basically nonmaterial. We can appreciate the words of Sir James Jeans, professor at Princeton and Cambridge and research associate at Mt. Wilson Observatory (1923–1944). In 1930, he said, "The stream of knowledge is heading toward a nonmechanical reality; the universe begins to look more like a great thought than a great machine." Physicist David Bohm added weight to this judgment in 1951, when he wrote of analogies between quantum processes and thought processes.[19]

By applying Sir James's simile to the dynamic dance of energy in the universe, we arrive at two important ideas about the cosmos. First, a thought is not a thing but a process. It is not like a cabinet or a painting that can stand free in its completed form; the thinking process and the thought continue together. A thought is not done once and for all, but changes as the thinker thinks. We know that the universe is not what it was a million years ago, or two thousand years ago, or at the beginning of last month. It is not only that scientists are still finding out new stuff about the universe, but that the universe itself continues to evolve and change.

Second, Sir James's idea suggests that Ultimate Reality cannot be far away, far beyond space and time. An artist can paint a mural and walk away, leaving his work in place to be enjoyed. A farmer can leave the field in which he has been working and let the processes of nature cause the seeds to sprout and the plants to mature for the harvest. But a thinker cannot leave her thoughts, those flickering patterns of energy weaving together to form the network of ideas. They cannot continue if she stops thinking.

One of the twentieth-century developments in theology is called process theology, which sees the process of God and the changing universe as producing new possibilities, as time goes by. (Or is it, perhaps, better to say, "As we move through time"? Who knows what time is?) The image, the metaphor for God that emerges, suggests an Ultimate that is dynamic, moving, working, and thinking. She is as close to us as we are to our thoughts about the people we love.

I try to use the female pronoun for God as much as I do the male. I am convinced that the male image has ruled the universe long enough. Our stereotypical ideas of God are off base. In spite of knowing better, we are influenced by pictures such as Michelangelo's, which portray God as a long-bearded white male. Surely the white image as well as the male image are both incomplete. It is absurd when people refer to God as "the man upstairs," but "the woman upstairs" is equally absurd. The animate world of any and all colors is both male and female, and the Ultimate includes both. (Actually, if I had to choose one, I think the image of the female would be

closer to truth, for in nature, the female in many species can reproduce without the assistance of the male, and maleness seems to exist
mostly to provide ways of allowing genetic changes in the offspring.)
In any case, the one-gender, one-race image is flawed. Of course,
every image is flawed, and we have to understand that. But it may
be that we should not think of God as a noun. Let me share another
idea with you.

Perhaps "God" Is a Verb

Benjamin Whorf, a former professor of linguistics at Massachusetts
Institute of Technology, held that the structure of the language we
speak also determines the way we think and therefore our view of
the universe.[20] English, along with German, Russian, Latin, Greek,
Persian, and Sanskrit, for example, share the same Indo-European
ancestry, but this does not apply to Chinese, Native American, Afri-
can, and other languages.

Besides sharing many common roots for important words, Indo-
European languages divide sentences into substantives (nouns or
pronouns) and the actions (verbs) that the substantives perform. We
supply the substantive even in sentences that don't require one. For
example, we say, "It's raining," or "It's a nice day." (*What* is raining? *What* is a nice day?)

In English we say, "The waves are rising." This implies that there
is an entity (a wave) that is doing something (rising). Yet actually
there is no wave until the rising happens, so *the rising is the wave*.
The subject and predicate are the same, the noun is the verb, but our
language disguises that. The Hopi, Whorf says, have a different approach, and they use one word that means something like "slosh."

Take another example. "A light is shining." Again, the reality is
that the *shining is the light*, and the *light is the shining*. So it is also
with "the fire is burning," which sounds as if there is a thing called
a fire that is doing something, namely burning. As in our previous
examples, however, *the burning is the fire*; there is no fire until there
is burning.

Suppose we apply these ideas to our concept of God. We have
tended to separate the Creator from the action of creating. Instead

of an Ultimate Reality that does something ("creates"), suppose that Creation and God are aspects of the same phenomenon, inseparable, like burning equals fire, shining equals light, or rising equals waves. Maybe the word for the Ultimate should be *Creationing*.

This would support the theological image that the universe is God's body. It would suggest that we see the "great thought" of Sir James Jeans as embodied in the vast mystery of the universe. The universe then becomes sacred, and the awe we naturally feel as we contemplate its unimaginable vastness would be the same as reverence. It might even add a sacred, rather than simply pragmatic or idealistic, dimension to our efforts to move toward ecological sanity.

Or Does "God" = "Universe"?

Astronomer Edward Harrison, whose book was cited previously, demonstrates that human beings have had many models of God, including the currently fashionable biblical model. We also have had many human models of the universe—attempts to say what the universe is. This includes the present-day widely accepted ideas of the Big Bang and relativity. We are aware that in times to come, our ideas of the universe will be superseded by new ideas and new understandings. Harrison comments:

> One may legitimately argue that as a result of rejecting the notion of gods, our views of reality have become pallid and inane, and our views of life itself devoid of satisfying and social meaning. Our cultural heritage impels us to believe in God or something similarly all-inclusive and inconceivable; for it has stolen from the phenomenal world the very elements essential for a life of significance and given these elements to the gods who have the function of sharing them with us . . . [W]hen we deny their existence and live in a godless universe, we are left with a residue of unfulfilled yearning.[21]

Mythologist Joseph Campbell expressed a similar thought in his TV series with Bill Moyers. Speaking of societies that decay when confronted with the technological world, Moyers says, "They go to pieces, they disintegrate, they become diseased. Hasn't the same thing happened to us since our myths began to disappear?"

"Absolutely, it has," says Campbell.

"Isn't that why conservative religions today are calling for the old-time religion?"

"Yes," Campbell replies, "and they are making a terrible mistake. They are going back to something that is vestigial, that doesn't serve life."

Moyers then recalls how the old myths, the "fixed stars" of his youth, told him that there was a kind, just father looking down on him, that his life was valuable, and that he had a known horizon. There was value in those ideas for a young man growing up. But now, Moyers comments, "Saul Bellows says that science has made a housecleaning of beliefs . . . I wonder what happens to children who don't have those fixed stars, that known horizon—those myths?"

Campbell responds, "All you have to do is read the newspaper . . . myths offer life models. But the models have to be appropriate to the time in which you are living, and the time has changed so fast that what was proper fifty years ago is not appropriate for today . . . [T]hat is what we are not doing. The old-time religion belongs to another age, another people, another set of human values, another universe."[22]

Both Campbell and Harrison are speaking of what someone has called "the God-shaped blank within us," saying that deep within the human psyche is a need for an idea of that which transcends us. We pay a price when we have a vacuum in that God-shaped blank. What can we find now in this age of quantum physics and relativity and technology? Harrison makes a suggestion.

He points out that both words, *god* and *universe*, refer to the utmost reality; both are all-inclusive, and both are unknowable to us in their fullness. So he refers to our human concepts as "universes" (lower-case *u*) and he refers to the real, the vast, the inconceivable, as "the Universe" (upper-case *U*). He applies the same principle to the deity. The idea of "god" means our human concepts and approximations. "God" is applied to Ultimate Reality—real, vast, inconceivable.

He therefore suggests that we at least speculate about the idea of the seventeenth-century Dutch philosopher Baruch Spinoza, who came to the conclusion that God and the Universe are one. This is not to say that God is in the Universe, or that the Universe is in God. They are both all-inclusive (nothing is outside God; nothing is outside the Universe); both are beyond human comprehension. Harrison ventures the name "UniGod," and says, "The Ultimate Reality we seek to understand by means of our universes is not a mechanistic world of dead matter that excludes the conceiving mind and all that we associate with the names of gods."[23]

Spinoza became a religious and intellectual outcast, condemned and rejected by Catholics and Protestants, and then by his own Jewish community. Even today he is shunned by philosophers. However, if we remember that he was speaking of a certain model of the universe and a certain model of God, maybe his ideas are worth restatement in this time and place.

Harrison says the end of the medieval universe, followed by the mechanistic universe of Newton and Descartes, has left our minds fluttering aimlessly amid the mechanisms.

> Belief in God or something similarly all-inclusive and inconceivable enables us to cling to a sane sense of proportion and view with equanimity the prospect that our universes are not the Universe and never can be. Belief in an unknown and unknowable God or Universe or UniGod at least counsels a sense of humility and reminds us constantly of the mystery of the inconceivable. In this way the gods within us will be placated.
>
> If we can think that all is far from known, and God is perhaps the Universe, then without further intellectual commitment we avoid the dreariness of atheism. By equating God and the Universe we give back to the world what long ago was taken away. The world we live in with our thoughts, passions, delights, and whatever stirs the mortal frame must surely take on a deeper meaning. Songs are more than longitudinal sound vibrations, sunsets more than transverse electromagnetic oscillations, inspirations more than the discharge of neurons, all touched with a mystery that deepens the more we contemplate and seek to understand.[24]

Harrison concludes that particular chapter by saying, in terms that are close to mythic:

> Do not deny the gods. Fight the gods if you will. But grovel and they will scoop you into the holy mincing machine of incarnadine wars. Hate them! Curse them! Though they may crush you, they will not despise you. But if you ignore them, then beware! For in their anger they will inflict on you nameless horrors of body and mind. Only fools deny the hereditary gods that live within us.[25]

As I understand him, we may legitimately stand against certain religious assumptions, certain narrow and aggressive theologies. We may be angry about them and oppose them. It may be that we lose such battles, but if we ignore this deeply human heritage, we pay a price. As Joseph Campbell says, we need only to read the newspapers to see some of those effects in a society that has cut itself loose from all ideas of the transcendent.

With no real sense of value inherent in the world and in its people, we have proceeded to develop a way of life that poisons itself by ambition and overreaching. We have lost all sense of the sacred in both the universe and in human relationships. Our society constructs a massive tower of materialistic grandeur that lacks the inner reinforcement of principles of compassion and humility. The danger is not that some external deity will proclaim judgment, but that the vacuum in the human heart will so weaken our effort that this unbalanced structure will fall from the very weight of its success.

Joseph Campbell's remarks in his series with Bill Moyers give us a thoughtful reminder:

> We have today to learn to get back into accord with the wisdom of nature and realize our brotherhood with the animals and with the water and the sea. To say that the divinity informs the world and all things is condemned as pantheism. But pantheism is a misleading word. It suggests that a personal god is supposed to inhabit the world, but that is not the idea at all. The idea is transtheological. It is of an indefinable, inconceiv-

able mystery, thought of as a power, that is the source and end and supporting ground of all life and being.[26]

Moyers asks if new myths might emerge from this image, and Campbell replies:

Well, something might . . . And the only myth that is going to be worth thinking about in the immediate future is one that is talking about the planet, not the city, not these people, but the planet and everybody on it . . . And what it will have to deal with will be exactly what all myths have dealt with—the maturation of the individual, from dependency through adulthood, and to the exit; and how to relate this society to the world of nature and the cosmos. That's what all myths have talked about, and that's what this one's got to talk about. But the society that it's got to talk about is the society of the planet. And until that gets going, you don't have anything.[27]

That's it. If we care, we must be willing to join the mythmakers.

The Meaning and Myth
of Being Human

Nowadays, we tend to use *myth* as a derogatory term; we see it as an account of make-believe beings in an unreal world. For those of us who take science seriously, that is an immediate barrier to taking myth seriously. Before we continue the course of our thoughts as we focus on the meaning of being human, we need to deal in at least a preliminary way with the meaning of myth. This is because we shall use both science and myth as we consider who we humans really are.

We often use the word *myth* to mean an untrue story or a mistaken idea. For example, we might say, "To present himself in a favorable light, the politician invented a mythical career in the air force." Or, "A major myth in the sports world is that nice guys never win." We may also use *myth* to describe a superstitious attitude: "The twenty-story hotel had no thirteenth floor because of the myth that thirteen is an unlucky number." Sometimes we confuse myths and fairy stories.

In every culture, people enjoy stories, and that includes myths. The original meaning of the Greek word *mythos* is "story." Unlike fairy stories that are designed basically to provide entertainment, though, myth seeks to deal with realities that elude capture in ordinary discourse. Myths are an attempt to make sense of human experience in the real world, pondering such questions as, Where did the universe come from? Who or what is in charge of it? Why are we alive? Why do we suffer? Why do we die? What is mortality? Why are we concerned about good and evil? What is morality?

Within a given culture, myths are generally accepted as true and as providing a real clue to understanding why things are as they are and how people should live. Nor are all myths from ancient times. In the United States, there was a mythical concept about the Old West; there were stereotypical good guys (white hats) and bad guys (black hats). Settlers and pioneers were good; Indians were bad. Until very recent times, a plethora of Western movies repeated these themes over and over, and the American people generally thought that the Western myth was true. They thought and acted on the basis of that view, though more recent writings and films have seen attempts to demythologize the Old West.

The first definition of myth in a respected dictionary is "a legend or story, usually something that attempts to account for something in nature. Most myths express religious beliefs of a people and are of unknown origin." Because in some cases we see myth as something false or untrue or fake, we belittle myths of religions other than our own. In fact, many of us feel that we must deny that there is anything mythical in our own tradition, fearing that to admit that it contains myth is to reduce its credibility.

The philosopher Salustius, in the fourth century of the Common Era said, "Myths are things that never happened but always are." Myths provide insight into many aspects of the universe and of human life, though they are more like metaphors or poetic images than literal records of events or relationships. Because they are stories rather than abstract concepts, they are easier to remember, and therefore provide patterns that enable human beings to enter into their varied experiences.

In fact, theologian Paul Tillich insists that whenever human beings try to speak of Ultimate Reality, they must use symbols and myths, because that is the only way creatures in space-time can think about that which is not in space-time. Tillich says that all stories in which the divine interacts with humans are to be considered mythological.[28] A god who enters into space-time is no longer the mysterious and ultimate "Power to Be," but a being among others. To use the metaphor from the previous chapter, the light of the projector has stopped projecting the images and has instead become one of the images!

Tillich urges "demythologization," by which he means that we must recognize a symbol as a symbol and a myth as a myth. A symbol points beyond itself to that which is symbolized, as a flag may symbolize the meaning and character of a nation (though obviously it is not the nation itself). The citizens of a country salute their own flag, and their enemies will burn that flag. A cross is a symbol of Christianity, the Star of David symbolizes Judaism, the crescent represents Islam, and the word *God* is a human symbol for the Ultimate, beyond definition and description. When we speak of God as involved in human life, in space-time, the representation is mythical, not literal.[29]

But many people are afraid of every attempt at demythologization. They resist any effort to point out the symbolic character of a story. Such opposition results in literalism. When this happens, Tillich asserts, creation is seen as a magical act that happened "once upon a time." The fall of Adam is located on a geographical point and is assigned to a specific person. The virgin birth is seen as a biological transaction, and the resurrection and ascension are described as physical events.[30]

Myths are vehicles of truth, but they are not facts. To repeat a point from an earlier chapter, the American Revolution was based on symbols and myth, not simply fact. The "self-evident truth" that all men are created equal and endowed by their Creator with the inalienable rights to life, liberty, and the pursuit of happiness is part of the myth that led Americans to found their nation. When that vision and those values are doubted and mocked, the structure of our living culture is endangered. That is why, as Joseph Campbell indicated, we need a new myth that will apply not just to the people of America, but to all the people of the planet. We need a story that all people can understand and incorporate into their vision of human life.

We do not know how or even if such a story may come to be. Nevertheless, it is important to realize that we are using myth and that our statements are not facts, but truth. We must be committed to facts as far as they are known, but our understanding, our story, our myth, must be more than a mere recitation of scientific knowledge—it must blend information and vision. But how do we do this?

Colin Tudge, a British science writer of excellent reputation, cites the work of Misa Landau who, in 1979, was a young historian of science at Yale. She was researching how anthropologists in the past century or two looked at the development of human life. The anthropologists perceived and portrayed the genus *homo* as a hero of the kind found in the folktales of every culture. Coming from a humble beginning, the hero faces a series of trials in which he is triumphant, and in so doing grows until he emerges as "intelligent man," *homo sapiens*. In many instances he then falls into the sin known to the Greeks as *hubris* (excessive pride) and faces destruction.[31]

Tudge comments that some scientists denied this observation and insisted that science merely sets forth facts. Others realized that Landau was correct, and they were shocked to see the mythlike structure in their own work. A third group, in which Tudge includes himself, effectively said, "All right. So be it." Tudge asserts that science progresses by not only theories but also by heuristic ideas; that is, ideas which, though not literally true, promote understanding and suggest testable hypotheses.

The concept of early humans as heroes is a coherent idea that gives an overall sense of what went on. Tudge says that the human mind enjoys stories and grasps their meaning, but he warns that there is a real danger in this: we imagine that the story is literal truth, whereas myth merely provides a framework on which the truth can be hung.[32]

With that as a given boundary and with the understanding that a myth is a story that should be taken seriously but not literally, we come to our discussions about how we human beings can think of ourselves.

What Are We?

What kind of creatures are we human beings anyway? The Bible maintains that we are made in the image of God, but what does that mean? We have already discovered that our concepts of God are inadequate. They may point toward God, but the Ultimate Reality itself is beyond our reach. Furthermore, human beings created their ideas of God in the image of human beings. Certainly the gods of Greek and Roman myth are like human beings, with their quarrels, their favorites, their rivalries, their egos. This is also evident as we look at the stories about Yahweh found in the Hebrew Scriptures. He is portrayed as surprised and angry at how human beings misbehave, so that in disgust he decides to destroy his creation by flood. After the flood he is sorry for what he has done and makes a promise, by means of a rainbow, that he will never do that again. In the Ten Commandments it is claimed that he is "a jealous God," and he tells his chosen people to "have no other gods before him."

So can it mean anything to say that we are "in the image of God?" Is there anything in us that resembles the Ultimate? We exist, along with galaxies and black holes, along with supernovae and stars and asteroids, photons and gravity. Human beings are not apart from the universe; we are a part of the universe that wonders and ponders, that looks at the universe and at ourselves and asks, "What are we?"

Does that make us special? Are there other parts of reality that try to peer through space-time and understand what it means? Once again, we must say, "We don't know." However, we can guess; many thoughtful people have begun to look out into the expanding mystery and ponder the possibilities of intelligent life in other places. They surmise that since there are billions of galaxies and each galaxy contains billions of stars, the chances are that somewhere among all those awe-full centers of energy that we call galaxies, there are planets containing beings who also wonder and ponder. We can surmise, but we don't know.

But of ourselves, we do know. We know that we wonder, that we try to understand who and what we are. We ask, "What does it mean, if anything?" The only answer to our question is an inner echo, ". . . anything?" Meanwhile, we look out into the immensity of space from our small blue planet and think about things. The universe itself does not answer us.

We also look about ourselves on the planet we call Earth, and we see that we are kin to the creatures around us; we are literally of the earth. We are made of the elements found in rocks and soil, in seeds and worms and molds and dung beetles. In fact, the molecules in our bodies have belonged to other creatures before they came to us. When we eat a pork chop or a leg of lamb, when we eat corn or spinach or beans, we turn molecules from pigs and sheep and plants into human molecules. The calcium we absorb from a hamburger becomes part of a human organism and we use it when we think, when we write or read.

Star Stuff

Scientists tell us that the atoms of the earth and all its creatures were formed in the interiors of great stars billions of years ago. When those stars died, their collapse formed the heavier elements as hydrogen atoms were changed into more complex atoms by intense pressure and heat. The dying stars exploded as supernovae and flung the heavy atoms of the new elements out into space. Gravity brought many of them together, eventually to become planets circling our sun and other stars.

All living creatures in this world and even the world itself are composed of the stuff produced by ancient stars. This sounds like the basis for a myth—human beings are descended from stars! However, this does not indicate any special status for humankind. This is a fundamental and pervasive process in the universe, and human beings are firmly rooted in the eons-long history of the cosmos that has produced the earth, the solar system, and all the galaxies. We are from this earth as well as the ancient stars.

Our very name for ourselves, *human,* proclaims that we are earthy. *Human* derives from the same ancient Indo-European root as *humus,* the essential soil for the growth of plants. And from that same linguistic root comes another important word, *humble,* meaning "close to the ground." We are as common as dirt!

Human beings are great-great-grandchildren of the stars and directly descended from the earth. We are not outsiders who come into the world; we come out of it, as a bud comes out of a tree. In this way we are related to all the life of earth—bacteria, amoebas, sponges and starfish, carp and sharks, worms and tigers, apes and hummingbirds. Biologists now tell us that even within our own human cells there are still living remnants of ancient microbial beings,

living and working inside the human organism (and in other creatures as well).

The mitochondria in the cells of most living beings, including
humans, seem to have been originally bacteria that invaded other
ancient organisms with nucleated cells (bacteria are not nucleated),
and entered gradually into a symbiotic arrangement that benefited
both. These mitochondria work semi-independently of the cell, di-
viding on a different schedule from the cell itself. They are the power-
houses that enable cells to change food into energy. We could not
survive without them.

Biologists think that the development of cooperative living (sym-
biosis) enabled many organisms to move more rapidly into new ways
of surviving and allowed for more varieties to develop. It seems that
we not only are akin to bacteria, but that we are blended with them.
Humans are directly involved with other earthly creatures.

Lewis Thomas, a physician affiliated with a well-known cancer
clinic, published many essays dealing with human life and the realm
of living things. A gifted writer, he presents scientific findings with a
flair for poetry and metaphor. The final collection of his essays is
entitled *A Long Line of Cells*. In the introduction, he says that whether
or not we like it, human beings go back to a single-celled bacterium
from some three-and-a-half billion years ago. (He interjects that
our more immediate ancestors in the 1800s were embarrassed at
being related to apes. He hints that knowing our bacterial rela-
tives would have probably totally destroyed their exalted human
self-image.)

Thomas says that despite numberless guesses, nobody knows
where that first single-celled parent came from. But in any case, all
the cells that came later—no matter whether plants, insects, mam-
mals, or even the cells of the human brain—carry the same strings of
DNA and follow essentially the same genetic code.[33]

Thomas further provides an informative insight into our continuing relationship with bacteria. We human beings can exist only
because we have the help of a tremendous number of bacteria who,
billions of years ago, swam into cells like ours and stayed there.
These "guest cells" replicate on their own schedule, and they are indis-
pensable: they assist in our basic life processes. Equally, they could not

live without us. We are bound together and live in intimate harmony.

Thomas also points out that from the perspective of the bacteria, the human body may be a sort of carapace, a shell, for the colonies of bacteria that live within us. Either way, the mutual accommodation works, just as it works for most other creatures in this world. The popular slogan for evolution, "survival of the fittest," sounds as if all the varieties of creatures are put in a big arena and ordered to fight it out in a bloody competition to the death. It turns out, however, that some of the fittest to survive are those who have learned to live in mutual cooperation. That learning has been a major engine in the growth of new and more capable creatures.

We return again to Fritjof Capra, this time to his excellent book, *The Web of Life*. He offers a quotation from Lynn Margulis, coauthor of the Gaia theory (that earth behaves like a living organism). She says, "Far from leaving microorganisms behind on an evolutionary ladder, we are both surrounded by them and composed of them . . . [We] have to think of ourselves and our environment as an evolutionary mosaic of microcosmic life. It is the growth, metabolism, and gas-exchanging properties of microbes . . . that form the complex physical and chemical feed-back systems which modulate the biosphere in which we live."[34]

Considering this deep involvement of organisms with each other in countless interdependent loops at almost every level, Capra writes that the scientific theory of symbiogenesis (the creation of new life forms through the merging of different species) is barely thirty years old. But, he points out that

> . . . as a cultural myth the idea seems to be as old as humanity itself. Religious epics, legends, fairy tales, and other mythical stories around the world are full of fantastic creatures—sphinxes, mermaids, griffons, centaurs and more—born from the blending of two or more species. Like the new eukaryotic (nucleated) cells, these creatures are made of components that are entirely familiar but their combinations are novel and startling . . . For example, the god Ganesha, who has a human body with an elephant head, is one of the most revered deities in India, worshipped as a symbol of good luck and a helper in

overcoming obstacles. Somehow the collective human uncon-
scious seems to have known from ancient times that long-term
symbioses are profoundly beneficial for life.[35]

Capra's book is an invaluable resource for anyone who seeks to
understand what life is and how it works. The new insights in biology are comparable to the development of quantum physics as a
new paradigm for scientific understanding. However, in this writing, we are simply considering ways in which we human beings can
understand ourselves.

Capra's citation of ancient mythical ideas about the production
of strange new creatures through combining characteristics of very
different species suggests again that truth may be set forth in myth,
though the ideas are literally untrue. As was mentioned earlier, Colin
Tudge reminds us that a myth about human origins can give us a
frame on which to hang new ideas: we can learn from it, though we
must remember that it is not literally true. Following that idea, let us
look at a very familiar biblical myth, namely, the creation of Adam
in the second chapter of Genesis, which was written perhaps in the
tenth century before the start of the Common Era. (The account in
the first chapter of Genesis is of later origin and treats the story in
quite a different way.)

In the second chapter of Genesis, we see an anthropomorphic
deity who walks upon the uninhabited earth; there are no plants,
though there is a stream of water. The author of the old story comments that the reason nothing is growing is that there is no one to till
the ground. In other words, Yahweh wants a gardener, someone to
care for the earth. Then Yahweh molds the dust, the clay (*adamah*)
into a man ("Adam"), and breathes into him the breath of life.

One aspect of this myth is that when God breathes the breath of
life into the clay of man, the new creature is literally inspired. The
Hebrew word for breath and spirit is *ruach*; likewise in Greek,
pneuma means both breath and spirit. Our English word *spirit* is
directly from the Latin word for breath, *spiritus*. So the invisible air
and the invisible spirit are from common linguistic roots, and we
still have remnants of that relationship in our common speech. For
example, a *gust* is a sudden stirring of air or wind, and a *ghost* is

thought to be a stirring of spirit. Our derived word *expire* means that both breath and spirit depart. These words show the long poetic association of these invisibles.

The old Adamic myth says that a human being is inspired clay. To be inspired means to get new ideas, to be motivated, to make connections. Man is the clay of the earth, the humus that gets ideas, that is motivated to explore and make connections. There are obviously other important aspects of the myth; Yahweh realizes that the man needs a suitable partner, so Yahweh creates all the creatures from the same dust as the man. Thus, we are clearly related to the creatures in the world. After the animals are made, the man names them. (We attach nametags to everything from quarks and electrons through seagulls and ostriches to planets and galaxies and the universe and beyond. Sometimes we forget that "God" is not God's name; it is simply our nametag for the Ultimate Mystery.)

None of the creatures, however, is a fit partner for man, so Yahweh makes the woman from material already in the man. In the first chapter of Genesis, male and female are created at the same time, brought into being by divine decree. A careful reading of the first chapters of Genesis is instructive; it enables the reader to contrast the two creation stories. They do not agree with each other and neither is literally true. (The people who, through time, assembled the books that came to be the Bible allowed much more variety than some of us would believe.)

The myth of Adam agrees with the scientific view that human beings and other creatures are made of the same materials as the earth, but we may get insights from the myth that we do not find in the scientific story. For example, the myth says that only humans lost their innocence by eating from the tree of the knowledge of good and evil; the other animate creatures did not "eat of the tree of the knowledge of good and evil." Sharks, tigers, tapeworms, rats— these creatures are often tagged by human beings as "bad," but they are not evil, even though the ways they work for a living do not make humans happy. They simply obey their nature.

This does not mean that animals cannot make choices; an elk may decide which clump of grass to graze first, or a squirrel may choose which apple to nip. A female bird may decide which of the courting males she will accept. There is increasing evidence that groups of animals have an accepted social order and rules that are established and enforced on the young until they know that there is a price to be paid for nonconformity. Nevertheless, only humans are equipped to make moral and ethical choices. Charles Darwin wrote, "Of all the differences between man and the lower animals, the moral conscience is by far the most important." He said that "conscience is summed up in that short but imperious word 'ought.'"

Sometimes people choose to defy the rules and leave the tribe. But human choices are more than obedience to tribal rules. A human being may choose to go on a complete fast for the sake of some moral principle. A human being can decide whether to respect the rights of other human beings or to use people for her own convenience. A human being can work for the betterment of the poor or weak. We increasingly see that ethics are deeply related to our attitude toward and participation in the realm of nature. Ethical standards are set by human beings and are applicable only to human beings.

From ancient times, people have debated the nature of good and evil. Philosophers disagree as to the nature of virtue. Is good an absolute quality, divinely established, or is it a subjective and relativistic human value? People have made persuasive arguments for both positions, and in either case, they desire that the hearer/reader choose the position they are presenting. They assume that their audience can decide, can choose.

Some philosophers assert that people really have no freedom, that attitudes are determined by culture and by training. However, those who hold that all such human values are the predetermined result of background and conditioning do not treat their own ideas as simply the result of conditioning. Even if they declare that all human actions are culturally determined, they still present their case as if the hearer can choose whether or not to agree with them. As Joseph Wood Krutch says:

> The most stupendous of (human inventions) was not of the wheel, or the wedge, or the lever, but the values by which (the human) has lived, and that the ability to act on, for example,

the assumption that loyalty is better than treachery even when both seem to give a practical answer to a given problem, is more significant than any other ability he has ever manifested. It is also to believe that, in the future as in the past, what becomes of (man) depends less on what machines he invents or what governments are imposed upon him than on what values he creates.[36]

To speak in a mythic manner, we may say that humans are clay that creates and chooses values. We are not perfectly free; we are influenced by our culture and by our personal histories, but still, we have real freedom. If that is not true, then people's choices and values are meaningless; the great plays and novels are also meaningless, and any idea of either good or evil is merely a ripple in the ocean of unavoidable fate. A Caligula or a Hitler are, like Gautama Buddha or Jesus of Nazareth, simply accidental products of their environments. If people cannot choose, then the idea of democracy is an illusion, and there is no difference between a totalitarian dictatorship and a representative government.

Like the physical universe that modern physics seeks to understand, where matter and energy are the same, and where light is both wave and particle, so the realm of being human is composed of paradoxical opposites. To be human is to be conditioned, but it is also to have freedom. Human ideas and choices affect the course of events and even the universe itself, and with freedom comes responsibility.

The myth of Adam holds that the very purpose of the creation of humankind is that the world needed someone to tend to it, someone to do the "gardening." To take the myth one degree farther back, God valued the world and produced a creature who was responsible for taking good care of it.

Because most of us are more comfortable with a less mythical and a more scientific approach, let us look at the human relationship with the world in more scientific terms. Contemporary ecologists say virtually the same thing as the myth. Human beings can change the world. In truth, we have radically altered the world, so that it is in danger of being less able to sustain life—even human life. The

resources of the world have been overexploited; for instance, defor-
estation is a clear and present danger. The decimation of forests
reduces the ability of the atmosphere to absorb carbon dioxide; this
in turn intensifies the greenhouse effect and promotes global warm-
ing. Furthermore, as trees are destroyed, the topsoil erodes, rivers
become silted, and the land becomes less productive. With the ad-
vent of the industrial age, we have polluted the air as well as the
water, and toxic wastes make vast areas of land and sea uninhabit-
able.

We are beginning to understand from growing scientific evidence
that human beings are destroying the very earth on which we de-
pend. Thus, we are being asked to reinvent our economic systems so
that we will cease to pillage the world for temporary benefit.

Scientist and author Fritjof Capra says:

> The power of abstract thinking has led us to treat the natural
> environment—the web of life—as if it consisted of separate
> parts, to be exploited by different interest groups. Moreover
> we have extended this fragmented view to our human society,
> dividing it into different nations, races, and political groups.
> The belief that all these fragments—in ourselves, in our envi-
> ronment, and in our society—are really separate has alienated
> us from nature and from our fellow human beings and thus has
> diminished us. To regain our full humanity, we have to regain
> our experience of connectedness with the entire web of life.
> This reconnecting, *religio* in Latin, is the very essence of the
> grounding of deep ecology.[37]

Religio (connectedness, binding together) is the source of our
word *religion*. There is a spiritual dimension in humanity, there is a
"breath from God" in our makeup, and this reminds us that we are
all called to take care of the earth of which we are part. We are
creatures who can and must choose. We are creatures who have values. As Joseph Campbell reminds us (cited in the previous chapter):

> Any myth that may come to us in the future will have to deal
> with what all myths have dealt with—the maturation of the
> individual, from dependency through adulthood, and to the exit;

and how to relate this society to the world of nature and the cosmos. That's what all myths have talked about, and that's what this one's got to talk about. But the society that it's got to talk about is the society of the planet. And until that gets going, you don't have anything.

We should restate that. "Unless that gets going, we won't have anything—not even ourselves." So, in a mix of scientific and mythic views, we can say this:

- The earth is made of elements recycled from the explosive deaths of great stars billions of years ago.

- From the earth came the materials of which the human body is made.

- Now in us, the ancient star-stuff has conscience and choice and plays a conscious and responsible role in the ever-changing universe.

Small though our role may be when it comes to the entire universe, it profoundly affects what happens on the small blue planet that we call home. That is critical for us and for all the other living things that share the world with us.

If we continue our mythoscientific perspective on humankind, we can imagine that human beings may cry out, "Hey, God! Things are getting pretty bad here! We face a lot of problems with the way we live and how to manage things. Why don't you do something?"

And God replies, "I have done it. That's why you are here, remember?"

What Difference Does It Make?

Our friends Julia and Sam had invited Nancy and me to join them at the neighborhood Chinese restaurant; they had coupons that would provide a price break on our dinners. We accepted gladly, since we had not seen them in several weeks. (Besides, we enjoy Chinese cuisine!) It was a Friday night and the small restaurant was quite full. The four of us chatted randomly about various subjects after we ordered. Just as we were finishing our egg-drop soup, Julia began to address Nancy and me in a more direct and focused way.

"Well, I can't wait any longer. One reason we wanted to share dinner with you is that we have some good news." She paused only briefly before she said, "We just found out for sure a couple of days ago; I'm pregnant!" She smiled broadly and leaned back from the table. Nancy and I reacted with genuine joy and extended congratulations and good wishes. Julia and Sam told us when the birth was expected, but they did not know yet whether it was to be a boy or a girl. "Really," said Sam, "we don't have a preference—just the hope that things will go well, that the baby will be healthy and normal."

The waiter came in with a trayload of savory entrees, put the tray on a folding stand, and placed the covered serving dishes on the table. He refilled our small teacups and moved on to another group of customers. We passed around the various entrees, dished out our portions, and began to eat again.

Once again, Julia spoke. "You know, it's funny, but I have suddenly begun to pay more attention to what the state legislature is doing. I realize that my baby is probably going to be attending school in this state, so I am especially interested in funding, in reorganizing the schools, and the level of education that our kids will receive. Hey, that's *my* kid who's going to be affected!"

We all agreed that we get more interested in politics when we can see direct ways in which the laws will change our lives. "Well, that's all to the good," Julia observed. "But I got interested in that proposal to post the biblical Ten Commandments in every school room. I had been watching that development with interest, mostly because I think that posting those religious rules is unconstitutional. But my pregnancy turned the general concern into a very personal one. How will I want my child to be schooled?"

"Yes," Nancy agreed. "We have the same concern about our grandkids. We see a lot of ugly tendencies in our society, so we share your worries. What kind of world will these little people grow up in?"

Sam spooned some more steamed rice onto his plate. "Yeah, I know. I really worry about the things we are doing to our world and to each other. What will we teach our little one when the time comes? Americans seem to be really ambiguous about standards and goals. I think, somehow, that we must start to think more seriously about what life is, and we surely want to give our kids some understanding of how to live, how to make decisions. At least posting the Ten Commandments would suggest some specific standards, wouldn't it? What do you think, Joe?" I saw this question as aimed at me not only because I was the oldest person in the group, but also (by virtue of owning a pulpit robe, unused now for several years) the supposed authority on requirements for living well.

"Well," I managed to say, "I don't think the posting of the commandments would have much effect on the lives of these kids. First of all, there are more and more kids in our nation who are not related to either the Jewish or the Christian tradition. They're coming from Islam, Buddhism, humanism, and paganism. So obviously, Julia is right; there is a real conflict with a constitutional amendment that favors one specific religion over others. But I have other concerns about that idea.

"The people who advocate posting the Ten Commandments have

a mistaken idea about words. Words are very powerful tools for human communication, but just having them posted does not mean they are effective. People run stop signs all the time, though they know well what that means. Signs with the speed limit displayed do not make people drive more safely, and the slogan, 'Don't drink and drive,' does not make drunks into sober drivers.

"If the legislators who advocate posting the Ten Commandments had really read the books containing those commandments, they would see that those same books later tell of murder, gang rape, and torture, even dismemberment. They recount brutal intertribal strife, genocidal horrors, the destruction of whole towns, and the slaughter of women and children. And later, even the kings broke the rules. King David of Israel committed adultery and ordered the general of his army to arrange the almost certain death of the soldier whose wife he coveted. People who lived under the authority of the Ten Commandments continued to steal, to murder, to break marriage vows, and to bear false witness. They even worshipped various pagan gods! So, knowing the words doesn't produce the results."

"But, Joe," objected Sam. "What you are saying is that there is no use in having laws or rules, because people don't pay attention anyhow. Isn't that a defeatist attitude?"

"It does get frustrating," I said. "We've all experienced that feeling that no matter what we do as individuals, there will be people who take advantage of others, people who hurt their neighbors and their communities. You can get pretty cynical if you let yourself. But strategies have to be planned and developed realistically. There have to be rewards for people who cooperate, and there have to be penalties for people who refuse to fit in. And we need such mundane things as locks on doors and police who can help enforce the laws. And of course we need a justice system to balance the needs of both individual and community. These issues will never be permanently solved, but I am confident that just tacking a poster of 'Thou Shalt Nots' to the wall will not solve our dilemmas."

"I agree with that," said Nancy. "But at the same time, I think there's a need for some central principles and ideas. We can't raise kids with just arbitrary rules made up by parents in individual families. You can't just say 'I'm the Mommie (or 'I'm the Daddy'), and do this because I say so.' I mean, even parents have to base their instructions and decisions on some principles broader than personal convenience. What ought we to teach kids so that they can get along in the larger society?"

All four of us sat silently for a few moments, enjoying our food and each other's company, thinking about Nancy's question. I imagined that they were looking to me to give an answer, though nobody said so. Then Julia, a practicing attorney, punctured my egotistical bubble. "Well, we can start with the rules of our society. Obey traffic laws. Don't take other people's things. Don't cheat. Don't hurt others. Aren't those good rules to teach?"

I was thinking as Julia talked, trying to sort out what she was saying. Finally I ventured, "I think we have two kinds of rules here. One kind is for safety or procedural matters. 'Stop at stop signs' is different from 'Don't steal,' or 'Don't cheat.' The first kind is like the rule not to touch a hot stove: it says that you need to be watchful for danger and look before you leap. On the other hand, rules about honesty or not hurting others deal with morality or ethics rather than personal safety."

"Oh, I don't know," said Sam with a deadpan look. "Not hurting others may be a way to avoid being socked when you make another person mad, right?"

"Ignore him," said Julia. "He's just pretending to be dumb, and he is very good at it! But I love him anyhow."

"Thanks for nothing," Sam grinned, but then he went on. "Nonetheless, isn't it true that many of our social rules exist for the purpose of the social system by lowering friction and providing a sort of safety zone around people? Aren't a lot of laws designed to enable people to live together?"

"Sure," Julia answered. "Rules like that vary from place to place and from time to time, depending on current social needs. In America, we drive on the right side of the street, and in England they drive on the left. Without rules, traffic would be too tangled up for anyone to get anywhere. Rules lubricate the social structure. The same is true of rules about noise and letting pets run loose and not throwing garbage onto the streets. Rules prevent disputes, and they help solve disputes when they arise anyway. And most of us gradually learn to take these rules seriously enough that we observe most of them most of the time."

"Yeah," said Sam. "We all need to learn the rules to survive in our own society. But things like the Ten Commandments are not just cultural rules, like which side of the street to drive on, or when or how you pay your taxes. They are more like general principles, aren't they? So if you are trying to teach your kid something more fundamental than local laws, or even state or national laws, what should you teach?"

I tried to respond to Sam's question. "I think that the basic principles are those that enable a society to survive. If a group should allow people to kill each other, the group could not survive. So murder is universally forbidden. Even wolves, hunting together as a pack, do not attack one another. I know of no social system that allows for murder, though in general a tribe allows its members to kill members of a different tribe under certain conditions, and sometimes the tribe itself may kill a member that has broken its major rules.

"Likewise, stealing from others in your group is frowned on in every human society. In general, people do not have to stand protectively above the necessities of life, like snarling hyenas defending their share of the kill. And perfidy and deceit are deadly viruses in any social system; there must be a certain level of trust among group members. It seems to me that we can and should inculcate these sorts of values in our kids: respect for life, especially human life; respect for other people's possessions; and honesty and straightforwardness. Does that make sense?"

"Well, yes," responded Julia. "It's great as far as it goes. But there are lots of other ideals in the Ten Commandments, aren't there? For example, 'Honor your father and mother.' That sets forth the obligation to respect parents, and so that helps hold the family together. And what about 'Remember the Sabbath Day, to keep it holy'? Aren't those ideas important?"

"Of course they're important," I said, "because they deal with deep matters. It is important for the family to be able to function, because the family sustains the children and teaches them what they need to know. The Sabbath Day was a very important part of the Jewish religion, and formerly it was very strong in the heart of American religion—though mostly it was about keeping Sunday sacred, not Saturday, the Jewish Sabbath. But the Commandments were surely not intended for the kind of market economy we live in now, and they were not intended for a predominantly non-Jewish population. Many of our businesses close for the weekend; some are open Saturday but not on Sunday. But others do a great volume of business on Sunday; it would cause a major overhaul in our economics if we took that commandment literally. But in any case, in general we do not observe the Sabbath. What would be the function of telling school kids in America that they had to observe the Sabbath?

"The fact is, the Ten Commandments are related to the Jewish faith system. They are not as universal as some people think. They grew out of the experience of Israel more than twenty-five hundred years ago. Consider not only the Sabbath, but also the injunction against making graven images and bowing down to them, and the command not to use God's name in vain . . . And by the way, what does that really mean? What is taking God's name in vain? There are lots of scholarly comments about that, but there is no universal agreement."

Nancy spoke up. "But aren't there some valuable ideas in those specifically Jewish rules? For example, having respect for your parents is important for kids in a humanist family, or a family from Siberia or Malaysia. And even though we don't all observe the Sabbath, isn't it good to have some time set aside for the spiritual life, whether it's for reading or prayers or meditation. Maybe our spiritual lives are impoverished because we don't take time out of our rat race in order to nourish the soul."

Nancy paused while she expertly filled and rolled a moo shu pancake. "And I think that not taking God's name in vain," she continued, "implies that we need to have some sense of the transcendent or the holy. Somehow, our society needs to have some awareness of reverence and respect. And that includes other people's religious practices and beliefs. If nothing is holy or sacred, then everything becomes . . . well, tawdry."

"Maybe so," said Sam. "But meanwhile, please pass the sweet-and-sour shrimp."

Since the requested dish was near me, I picked it up and handed it on to Sam. "I think you are absolutely right about that. I think our society suffers a lack of vision, a lack of values. But I still think that tacking up a poster of the Ten Commandments won't do what's needed. The whole issue needs to begin with individual people and individual families. The schools can do some of it—respect for others, the wrongness of murder and theft, the need for honesty. Those values are pertinent in almost all religious traditions. But how people understand and practice their faith is a private matter. Ideas of God—or whatever you want to call the Ultimate—cannot be left to the public schools. And most specifically, Sam, when your little one gets to the stage of learning about values and virtues, you and Julia have to be responsible for that. That doesn't mean that you can't rely to some degree on Sunday school or church to help; in fact, they can be important resources. But you have to determine what kind of faith system you want your child to grow up with.

"One of our big problems in America is how to develop faith systems for life in a secular and contradictory world. If we do not believe that God directly gave us the rules, what kinds of rules and principles are really important for our survival? What kind of ethical system can we all honor in a society that contains many religions? And what things can we teach our kids so that they will respect the people around them?"

"Are we talking about what individual families can teach, or what kinds of laws our nations and states should have?" asked Julia. "Our national laws already leave it up to families."

"That's true," Nancy said. "The constitutional idea is that the nation cannot favor one religion over another, and that the law cannot keep people from practicing their own religious values."

"The answer," said Julia, "is not to try to establish national or state laws to tell people what to teach their families. It is to decide what we will teach our own children about living with people of many faiths and backgrounds. What can we teach that will equip youngsters to behave in ethical ways without becoming self-righteous?"

"That's right, Julia," I said. "We are responsible for determining our own basic values and teaching them in our own families. But in reality, we may be closer to people of other faiths than we think. Let me start with Judaism and Christianity to illustrate the point.

"The New Testament says that a fellow Jew asked Jesus what was the greatest commandment, and Jesus answered by quoting the book of Deuteronomy: 'Love the Lord your God with all your heart, with all your mind, and with all your soul. This is the first and greatest commandment.' Then he added, 'The second is like it: Love your neighbor as yourself,' a quotation from Leviticus. And Jesus said, 'On this hang the Law and the Prophets.' In other words, every other rule in the Scripture is based on these two principles.

"Let me rephrase those to fit our own age: First, love the highest truth you know, without hypocrisy. And then, treat your neighbor as you would like to be treated. You will find similar ethical statements in all the great religions, not just Judaism and Christianity, but also Islam, Buddhism, Taoism, and Brahmanism. These two essential principles, if we taught and practiced them in our homes, would do much to lower the tensions among us and to improve the civil climate. And it is just such principles that we really can teach and model in our families."

"Good!" said Sam. "I hate for us to get stuck with all the arbitrary rules made by human beings!"

"No kidding," said Julia. "My profession, law, exists because most of the rules and laws are technical and picky and hard to understand. But mostly they are not so broad or so deep that human existence depends on them."

"Sure," I said. "That's true. But step back a bit. Why do we need laws? What is it that drives not only the interpretation of laws, but also the making of them? Is there something more fundamental at the foundation of all the lawmaking?"

"Well," said Julia, "it's hard to define, but I think the basic need for laws and lawyers is that a society cannot exist without rules."

"In other words," said Nancy, "every game has to have rules. The rules for baseball are different from the rules that apply to bridge. And even hide-and-go-seek has some accepted rules about who is 'it,' and how the one who is 'it' has to give people a chance to hide, and stuff like that. There are rules if you want to play the stock market or golf or if you want to buy and sell real estate."

"That's right!" I said. "You are both saying that there is a sort of basic but unwritten law that any sizable group of people will need laws. Is that right?"

Julia and Nancy nodded assent, while Sam merely looked attentive.

"So if we were to try to put that in the form of a universal principle, we might say that one basic rule is that rules are needed. Lawlessness is not freedom, it is chaos. And people cannot function together in chaos. That basic rule is not something that was passed by legislators or pronounced by God; it grows out of the realities of human life."

"Yeah," said Sam, "but that is so abstract. How do you teach that to people, especially kids?"

"If you see that as a general rule you must follow the rules, you will set an example by living that way. And that principle applies to an individual family as well as to a town or a country. No given rule is ultimate, but the need for rules is very strong. And this implies that parents can and must establish some rules for the family. Kids need structure."

"Ah," said Sam. "I have another idea. In my field we try to keep up with the scientific work that makes our technology possible. And I know that in science and technology there are lots of rules. There are patent laws, for example, and people are not allowed to steal someone else's ideas. But there is at least one rule that is more basic than that. It seems to me that the whole undertaking of scientific research depends on every scientist and every researcher keeping one essential rule. That rule is, 'You must be honest.' Science depends on honest research, honest evaluation, honest reporting. It cannot advance on falsehoods, and cheaters will be discovered. That rule is not a law passed by a legislature; it is a virtue demanded by the universe itself. Otherwise, science could not exist, much less advance."

As we poured another round of tea, Julia commented, "It seems to me that there is a hierarchy here: on lower levels, there are rules for games like chess or baseball; then there's a level that enables society to function better, such as traffic laws. But there are other rules that are intrinsic to the very universe, like the rule against cheating in science."

I added an idea. "The big issue for any couple raising kids is to work out the really important principles and values they want to build their family on. For example, how do you learn about not cheating? You learn it in childhood games; you learn that it's more fun if you win honestly. And kids learn from their parents: we don't cheat in our taxes or in paying our bills. Honesty, fairness, kindness, and consideration grow out of family experiences. These are modeled by the family in mutual love.

"Children learn about accepting and honoring human differences from parents who do not disparage people who are different. They see their parents respecting justice and honest and open views of truth. They know whether their parents are cleaning up trash or leaving trash. And if the parents honor the search for the spiritual dimension of life, the youngsters will honor it too. But the important thing is how they live, how they relate to each other as a family. Each parent must embody what it is to be a loving human being."

"Sure," said Julia. "The only way the baby will learn about love is if we really live by love in our daily lives. Say you've spent your whole life in a monochromatic world, and then one day someone tells you, 'Look for the red car,' or 'Hand me the green sweater.' You won't have a clue about what that means because you've never seen color. So a baby needs to see love and honesty before you can teach it about love and honesty. It will see what the parents honor as important values, and it will probably ask questions.

"And for Sam and me, as we get ready for the big event and the little person who is coming with it, we have to think about these things now. We are really trying to pattern our lives by our principles. If we think the Ten Commandments are 'it,' then we need to understand those commandments and what they mean. If we think that other values are important, the same thing applies. We teach more by example than by word."

"Agreed!" Sam joined in. "But I guess my question still is, given the kind of ideas we hold—respect for science, but believing that there are many things that science does not address—or let me put it another way: we want a faith that is strong enough to affect our lives but flexible enough to change and grow as our lives unfold. With this kind of faith and value system, how shall we live?"

"In other words," said Julia, "if we have a more open belief system, is there a way to summarize its ethical demands?"

I paused before trying to answer. "I don't think I have ever tried to pin it down that way, partly because different situations demand different responses. The basic ethical principle is, I think, the responsible use of freedom. But then the question is, responsible to whom and why? The idea in the Ten Commandments is that humans are responsible to God as portrayed in the Bible; I think that we are responsible to ourselves and to the reality of which we are a part."

"Wait a minute," Julia said. "That can be pretty dangerous, can't it? After all, the Nazis were following their own reality when they set up the death camps and murdered Jews and Gypsies and gays on a wholesale basis. Can't we do better than that?"

Her words were sobering reminders. Ethical standards are easily twisted when self-interest is involved. "You're right, Julia," I said. "I don't know of a way to deny that. But let me try to deal with your objection, which, by the way, is absolutely valid.

"I still do believe that imperfect human beings are the source of our rules and laws, so laws are often twisted and warped. But the problem is that when people assert obedience to God as their unswerving highest value, we don't gain much. Look at the Inquisition: the Church was absolutely committed to furthering the rule of God, and in his name they tortured, burned alive, and persecuted untold thousands. Pogroms against the Jews were launched by people who thought of themselves as loyal Christians. In fact, the Nazis' hatred of Jews grew out of that long-practiced 'Christian' tradition of blaming Jews for everything bad in the world. So religious standards in no way guarantee justice or peace. In fact, fanatical adherence to certain so-called absolute standards are oppressive under extreme circumstances."

Across the table, Nancy raised her eyebrows in alarm. "Like what circumstances?" she asked.

"Take, for example," I replied, "Dietrich Bonhoeffer, a conservative Christian minister who opposed the Nazis. He was imprisoned for his opposition, and he later supported a scheme to assassinate Hitler. He was executed for that futile attempt. My point is that even he found it necessary to violate the religious standard against murder in order to try to eliminate a greater evil. So there is no set of rules that is invariably right. I believe that the only abiding principle is the rule of selfless love and the desire for what is best for all people."

"I agree," Julia said. "Sam's statement about the need for honesty in science is like that. Such rules are indisputable and inarguable when we view them against the backdrop of that principle."

The waiter came to our table with a plate of fortune cookies and the check. Sam took the check. "Well, one thing is for sure: you are our guests tonight, as we told you in advance." He placed his credit card and the coupon on the table, and the waiter took them off to settle the account.

While he was gone, we broke open our fortune cookies. The slip in mine said, *Tomorrow you will learn something new.* "That's good," I said. "I can always use that!"

Nancy's fortune read, *Your silence can speak volumes.* "I guess I can't say much about that," she observed.

Sam's slip averred, *You must think things through.* "Hmmm," he said. "The Universe has obviously been eavesdropping! What does yours say, Julia?"

With great ceremony, Julia unfurled the tiny roll of paper. Immediately her face lit with a grin. *You will find that you are filled with nice surprises,* she read.

With the shared laughter of that moment, we knew that the night's conversation was like our good Chinese dinner: deeply satisfying and enjoyable, but later we would want more.

Matters of the Spirit

When a person or a couple experience life-changing insights, by definition they must make some changes in the way they live. If their search for a faith makes no difference in how they live, they have probably not searched far enough or long enough. Julia and Sam had not only decided to think seriously about what are generally called "matters of the spirit," they had also learned that they were about to become parents. If there is one truism that is really true, it is that babies change the lives of the parents! It has even been said that if parents really knew how much babies would change their lives, the birthrate would be cut by two thirds. In any case, new parents find that their patterns of sleep, work, play, their sex life, the ways they spend money, and the ways they think of the future all change dramatically.

Sam and Julia are thinking more seriously about what the legislators are doing. They are finding that having a faith commitment demands some new thinking and probably some new reading and talking. They may find that various kinds of workshops seem to be worth attending; they are already thinking about what their real values are. They wonder how and what they will teach the new baby. With their liberal approach to faith and lifestyle in general, there is no simple set of rules to follow. Rather, they must earnestly seek to clarify who and what they themselves really are. They know that life decisions are frequently ambiguous, and they may often be unsure. Yet, they know that they must assume responsibility even when they do not know outcomes. They are resolved to be tolerant of the different attitudes about life that they find in the world around them.

Tolerance is, of course, one of the central virtues of the liberal outlook, but they will discover that it is not a panacea. Tolerance cannot be indifferent to demands for justice or ethical behavior, and practicing tolerance can sometimes be very painful.

The Limits of Tolerance

We who value tolerance sometimes behave as if we think tolerance is the ultimate value of the liberal spirit, a cure for all the ills of society. But, *tolerance always has limits, and ultimately, tolerance ends in intolerance.* For example, we may tolerate wide differences in lifestyle and religious practice. We allow people to follow their own faith even if it is not congruent with ours, as long as they do not demand that we subscribe to their philosophy. If they insist that women may not participate in the public life of their church, then their church is the loser, but if the women do not object, we feel that we can ignore it. If they demand that men wear long beards, or that all members refrain from wearing bright colors, or that women veil themselves in public, again we may wonder how anybody can subscribe to such ideas, but we agree that they can do what they want.

Tolerance can allow for a wide range of beliefs and practices, provided that we come from basically similar cultures. But what if your next-door neighbors come from a part of the world where nuptial rites call for sacrificing a goat and draining its blood on the ground? What if their homeland custom demands that the man beat his wife if she does not obey him quickly enough?

There is a limit to tolerance within our own culture in America. For most liberal-minded folks, gay and lesbian people are respected and welcomed; so are neighbors of different races. We welcome Jewish neighbors, Gentile neighbors, Muslim neighbors, Christian neighbors, as well as black, brown, or white neighbors. But what about neighbors who are skinheads or neo-Nazis, and what about those whose religion condemns all other spiritual practices and who strive for a society governed by their own narrow vision? Shall we ignore their efforts?

Some zealous religious believers often do a great deal of good in charitable projects; they may be honest, trustworthy, and lovingly concerned. But do we allow them to capture control of the local school board so that they can censor the scientific curriculum?

The paradoxical ethical reality that we must face is this: tolerance is not endless, and ultimately, *tolerance cannot tolerate intolerance.* As we decide to live our faith, whatever the specific content of the commitment, we must make a variety of interconnected decisions, and each person and each family must follow its own personal integrity. Along the way, some things become clear:

- If any human society is to survive, it must have agreed-on rules.

- In general, it is better to follow the rules, but in some situations we must break them in order to honor a higher principle.

- The proscription against murder must be a high priority.

- We must respect others' rights to their possessions and be honest in our day-to-day lives.

- We must respect marriage and partnerships.

- The ability to trust your companions is a fundamental principle of survival.

- Integrity is essential: we grow spiritually when we act from inner authenticity in all situations.

Situation Ethics

In 1966, Episcopal priest Dr. Joseph Fletcher published a book entitled *Situation Ethics*.[38] The book was both roundly condemned and highly praised. Some thought it was not stringent enough in setting forth a specific moral code. Others, however, saw it as a watershed work in clarifying moral theology.

Fletcher distinguishes three approaches to making moral decisions, and although his system grows out of the Christian tradition, it can work as a guide for non-Christians as well.

(1) *The legalistic stance* approaches any decision-making situation with a whole set of interlocked rules and laws. These laws are not guides, but demands for obedience. Since life is complicated and situations change, there are multitudes of additional subrules. Fletcher observes, "Statutory and code law inevitably piles up . . . because the complications of life (and the claims of mercy and compassion) combine . . . to accumulate an elaborate system of exceptions and compromises, in the form of rules for breaking the rules!"[39]

(2) *Antinomianism* (against all laws) approaches every situation afresh and without any general principles: you just make it up as you go along. It is totally unpredictable and it cannot be called an ethical system, for it has no way to think of what might be better or worse and no approach to right or wrong.

(3) *Situationism* acknowledges the rules and principles of the tradition in which it seeks to operate. These rules may illuminate every decision. Yet, the situationist is ready to modify or compromise if the situation demands it. He allows the function of reason and natural law; he acknowledges the high values of scripturally based ethics. But the situationist abides by one central value, namely, love of neighbor. She acknowledges that circumstances alter cases; she knows that a specific situation may demand an unusual decision, and she asks, "What does love say should be done here?" The

basic strategy is to apply love (or the highest good) to the situation, and reach a decision within that context.

Love, the commitment to the highest good for all, is not to be bartered away. Keep in mind that love for other people is not a feeling; it is an attitude by which we approach choice, and it serves as the guiding principle in making ethical decisions.

Let us consider, as an example, the heroine of the apocryphal Book of Judith.[40] It is set in the time of the Assyrian conquest of Israel, about 720 BCE. Judith is a wealthy and pious widow. She is diligent in prayer, obedient to the rules of mourning, observant of the dietary laws, and considered a saint by the people around her. When her town is surrounded by enemy troops under General Holofernes, Judith executes a daring plan: she dresses herself beautifully and makes her way to Holofernes' camp. She is taken to the general by guards, and she (1) lies to gain his confidence, (2) flatters and flirts with him, (3) gets him drunk so as to (4) seduce him into thinking he can sleep with her, and when he is in a stupor, she (5) cuts off his head. At the end she is regarded not only as a saint, but also as a savior-heroine.

Judith set aside her personal piety and natural obedience to rules in order to save the people of her village, and her story illustrates that when ethical principles are in conflict, one must choose the way that will benefit the most people. There is no such thing as a flawless set of rules that will always give an error-free answer to ethical problems, but this principle can give guidance even in complex situations.

Our goal from the beginning of this book has been to show that real life is complex and far from certain. Yet we have many responsibilities, and although the universe is not fair, we can seek fairness and justice in our relationships. We are star-stuff with power to make decisions; we are a part of the Universe that can make decisions and try to bring order out of its perplexities. It will not be done for us; we must do it ourselves. And that is how we live.

On Evil and the Devil

In American religion, evil and death are flies in the sauce of life, spoiling our ability to enjoy it. Many people think of death as evil, but this is a misperception. Death is simply related to the process of living; when the process of living ceases in any individual being, from alligator to zebra, that being is dead. Death may cause deep pain to humans and other living creatures, but it is not evil. Evil is related to human freedom and the making of human choices. *To the best of our knowledge*, only human beings make choices between right and wrong, but all living creatures are subject to death.

Apparent Evil Among Animals

We know of no other beings other than humans that choose evil. Generally, animals do not make a career out of killing their fellows, or constantly seek devious ways to harm other members of their own species. However, we may observe some apparent exceptions in the animal kingdom. Every so often television programs dealing with the subject of nature show a new male leader of a pride of lions killing cubs produced by the mating of the preceding leader, or sometimes a chimpanzee seizing a baby ape and killing it. The rest of the group seems upset, but they do not intervene. To us, it appears that an individual animal deliberately commits an antisocial action.

Ethologists surmise that sometimes the males of various species kill infants that are not their own as a way to ensure that their own genes survive while those of their rivals do not. Humans watching this spectacle may be shocked, thinking that animals engage in the same sort of notorious behavior of which they themselves are capable. However, ethologists conjecture that it is instinctual animal behavior, a natural strategy to eliminate a rival set of genes. We really do not know how conscious other creatures are of their actions—we can only make informed guesses.

Bad Doesn't Always Mean Evil

But we do know that human beings make moral choices. Some people choose to live outside the rules of their society so that their actions become a matter of habit and character. We may identify such individuals as bad people.

We have said earlier that there is no set of specific rules that must be applied universally. It often takes careful thought and evaluation to reach a decision; there are few perfect solutions. Certainly, sometimes even well-intentioned people make bad decisions, but bad decisions are not necessarily wicked or evil. Wrong decisions can be found in any human system, but that does mean that the world is wicked, nor does it mean that most people are bad.

There is an important distinction between *bad* and *evil*. For example, we may say, "This is really a bad storm," or "I had a bad day at the office." This does not imply moral lapses. People may say that a man-eating tiger is bad and must be killed, but it is not evil or wicked. Nor do we say that a storm is evil, for *evil* indicates a wrong intention, a warped will, a twisted attitude. Earthquakes, or avalanches, or volcanic eruptions may indeed wreak havoc and may kill hundreds or even thousands of people, but they have no evil intent. In fact, they have no intent of any kind. They simply exist and their existence may harm human beings.

The realm of nature, from microbiology to cosmology, does not intend either good or evil. The natural world simply exists. A tornado may destroy a church building and kill people within it, and so also may a bomb planted by a skinhead. The destruction may be total in either case, and the victims equally dead, but the tornado does not intend to destroy property or lives. The bomber is *evil*; the storm system is not. *Nature has no moral dimension.*

But there still are some people who see natural events as having moral meanings and destructive natural forces as evil. Whether they know it or not, they are echoing the teaching of the Persian prophet Zarathustra. Zarathustra, or Zoroaster, lived about six hundred years before the Common Era. He taught that there were essentially two deities, Ahura Mazda, the creator of good, and Angra Mainyu, the creator of all evil. The faith of Zoroaster was strong in Persia, the superpower of its time. Through the spreading influence of Persia, these teachings entered the thought-patterns of other peoples—Jews, Christians, and, later, Muslims. It still is strong in twenty-first century America.

[handwritten margin note: Christian Era]

Zoroaster and his followers believed in two nearly equal deities who sought opposing goals. Later, the view that a co-deity sponsored and promoted evil in the world strongly influenced the developing Christian view of the devil as a source of evil. For example, see *The Oxford Dictionary of World Religions* [41] and its article on Zoroastrianism. Jews and Christians became influenced by Zoroastrian teachings (especially those about the end of the world, the resurrection, and heaven and hell). The long-range effect is as if the Christians had baptized the evil Zoroastrian deity Angra Mainyu and turned him into the Christian persona of Satan or the devil. Evil in the universe was attributed to him.

Furthermore, in the milieu in which the early growth of Christianity took place, popular ideas of philosophy encouraged the notion that the physical world was a battleground of contending spirits. The letters of St. Paul and other New Testament writers confirm this. For example, in Ephesians we find: "Put on the whole armor of God, so that you may be able to stand against the wiles of the devil. For our struggle is not against enemies of flesh and blood, but against the principalities, against the powers, against the world rulers of the present darkness, against the spiritual hosts of wickedness in the heavenly places." [42]

People believed that above the earth was the moon, then the sun, then beyond that the stars, then the ethereal world of God and perfection. But between the moon and the earth, the space was filled with varieties of spirits, usually hostile to human beings. New Testament scholar Paula Fredriksen writes: "The moon marked the boundary of . . . permanence, stability, and harmony which characterized the astral sphere. In the sublunar realm matter grew thick and sinister; the air between the moon and the earth held demons and various spirits; chance, change and fate ruled life on earth."[43] Contemporary seekers can no longer believe in that model of the universe, and the Zoroastrian theology does not fit in the twenty-first century.

Nature Did Not Go Wrong

The realm of nature is not evil; though it contains much violence and pain, it also contains much beauty and inspiration. Despite its terror and wonder nature is value-neutral. It is we human beings who attribute good and evil to it. Where did we get the idea of evil? From Zoroaster? From the concept of original sin? From long-held tales about Satan or the devil? Long ago, the cartoon character Pogo said, "I have met the enemy, and he is us." Human choices produce evil in the world. From the myth of the Garden of Eden has come the notion that humans are tainted with original sin. The truth of the myth is that the freedom to choose (eat of the fruit of knowledge of good and evil) permits us to select evil over good, good over evil. Evil comes not from demons and devils, nor from original sin, nor from some rebellious part of nature.

There are plenty of things in the natural world that human beings see as repulsive. Nature is not automatically beneficent, and its processes do not particularly favor what people call morality or justice. Consider, for instance, the ichneuman fly. Many kinds of ichneuman flies (really wasps) deposit their eggs in other insects or spiders, converting the host into a living food factory for their young, which proceed to eat the host from the inside. The host continues to live for some time until finally the ichneuman's larvae have excavated their way through its tissues, usually avoiding the essential organs such as the heart, which are needed to keep the victim alive. The young flies are thus provided with a supply of fresh food until they are ready to leave the empty shell of the host and continue the life of their species. We might almost believe that Angra Mainyu indeed had been busy creating an evil set of creatures!

But the fly has no choice in the procedure; like a tornado, it simply *is*. Through thousands of generations these creatures have developed into what they are, with never an ethical decision being made. The viruses that afflict us, the bees that sting, and the sharks that bite are not making decisions to be evil. They may be dangerous but they are not evil

The Universe Does Not Exist for Us!

People correctly say, "The universe is not fair." Ultimate Reality is indifferent to human ethical standards. This point of view asks us to reconsider our ideas of God. Did God design the world? Are such creatures as the ichneuman flies, HIV, or the Black Plague compatible with perfect goodness? Would it not be possible to have a world without parasites? Viruses? Plagues? Let us consider our perceptions of the Ultimate.

In earlier chapters we thought of some alternatives to seeing God as a very big, powerful, and invisible superhuman. For instance, we could think of the Ultimate as being essentially the same as the Universe (Edward Harrison, Spinoza), or we could think of God as the thinker of the "great thought" which is the Universe (Sir James Jeans). Or we can consider God as a verb rather than a noun (Benjamin Whorf). Remember: any attempt to say what God is will be in metaphors, not direct descriptions.

In any case, the universe includes things that are horrific and destructive—supernovae and meteorites and black holes, parasites and predators, viruses and cancers. The universe includes murderous male chimpanzees, deadly plagues, and devastating earthquakes. The Mystery that some call God has produced a vast part of existence that we do not cherish. Though we are a part of it, the universe does not exist primarily for the sake of us humans.

There are deep problems with the common idea that God is "nothing but love," or "perfect love." The Taoists remind us that many things can be understood only in relationship to their opposite quality. If we did not know of dry, then wet would mean nothing. Dark and light help define each other; so do hard and soft. So do male and female. So do good and evil, and long and short. The Tao includes all these and other opposites. *Ultimate Reality is the One-ness that holds all opposites together in a universe that is all-inclusive.*

Let us look at a completely different attribute and see how it corresponds with our ideas of good and evil. *Up* and *down* seem to us to be easily understood and mutually exclusive opposites. Now imagine that we have a rocket at the North Pole, ready to be launched straight up, and then let us place an imaginary rocket at the South Pole, also ready to be launched vertically. Both rockets are success-fully sent on their ways and off they go, *in opposite directions. Up* from the South Pole is a different direction from *up* at the North Pole. *Up* has no meaning that extends to the universe. The light from the sun doesn't come *down* to the earth, though we see the sun as above the earth. Up and down have no significance in four-di-mensional space-time.

And yet for us in the world, up and down are important. When you fall, you fall down, not up. Up and down are very real in the world and make a difference in how we live, but they are irrelevant to the cosmologist. They are real and important, but they are local-ized meanings. Ultimate Reality includes evil as well as good, but that does not mean that the differences between good and evil are unimportant. It means they are earthly and human concerns and part of our human perspective.

God is not involved in our three-dimensional world in the same way that we are. For example, as we look down the length of a railroad track, it appears to get narrower and narrower as it gets farther away, but if we walk down that track, we discover that it does not get narrower as it is farther away. If we could be at both ends of the track at the same time, we would see that reality is differ-ent from our perception of it.

But that does not mean that the perspective of diminishing size with distance is a flawed way of seeing. In fact, we could not survive in our own three-dimensional space if things looked exactly the same size no matter how far from us they might be. That appearance of smallness with distance enables us to judge how far we must walk, how wide the chasm is, how fast the distant automobile is approach-ing. The apparent diminishing of size with distance is of great survival value to us as a species.

Freedom, Choices, and Ethics

For people in a social group, the difference between right and wrong may mean the difference between surviving and falling into total chaos. For human beings trying to live in the presence of other human beings, it is vital to be able to try to judge between evil and good intentions. We do not always choose correctly, but we know that choices count.

Choices *do* count. Evil results when human beings choose to use their power, their skills, their tools and implements to injure, harm, dominate, or mistreat human beings and other creatures in the world around them. When they use the hammer to kill a person instead of to build a house, that is evil. When they use trust as a way of cheating another person rather than a way of opening relationships, that is evil. When they use the power of the mind to defraud others, to gain power over them, or to take their substance, that is evil. Human beings have the power to debate with themselves internally and decide how they will help or harm their fellows.

We must bear in mind that evil is not always a violent threat. Evil intentions can motivate the smooth politician, the successful con artist, the gold digger, or the womanizer. Evil can assume the mask of the minister or the priest or the scoutmaster; evil can assume the friendly mask of a dealer in real estate or securities. The mask may be that of the convivial partygoer who chooses to drink and drive. Evil, whether embodied as a bloody murderer or a smooth-talking fraud, is present when human beings choose to use their own powers to harm others or put them at risk.

Because we all have freedom to choose, we are all subject to the possibility of doing evil. Within ourselves we have what Carl Gustav Jung calls "the shadow," the potential to do the unthinkable. Normally we try to suppress any impulse that is not socially or morally acceptable. Sometimes we try to *repress* an impulse, to bury it so deeply we are not even aware of its dark existence. Repressing the shadow does not make the energy disappear; the right trigger may cause it to explode in violent action. In some individuals such repressed compulsions may feel like an outside force—a devil—tempting them to do things that they try to resist.

Such hidden inner powers may take over an entire people: the ethnic carnage in Rwanda and in the former Yugoslavia in the last decade of the twentieth century are examples of such a group shadow. Such social evil also infected the Nazis, when Hitler's dark choices seduced frustrated people into joining with him to destroy other groups of people. Human choices lead to oppressive governments, to racist or ethnic hatreds, to mob violence and wars.

Freedom for Good and for Evil

Evil comes directly from human freedom. Human freedom produces the calculating terrorist who plants a bomb in an airport, a marketplace, or a schoolyard full of children. But virtue also arises directly from human freedom. Human choice produces a Mother Teresa or a Mahatma Gandhi. This is another important paradox: *good and evil come from the same source and neither is possible without the other.* The only way that there can be genuine goodness (embodying honesty, compassion, love, and so on) is that there be genuine choice. True choice demands the real possibility of choosing to commit evil or embody virtue.

Suppose, for example, a man thinks of robbing a bank; but when he arrives at the bank, he discovers that there are a dozen well-armed guards keeping watchful eyes on the situation. He sees that his chances of success are nil, and destruction of any transgressor is certain. If he keeps his gun hidden and creeps quietly out of the bank, he has not suddenly made an ethical choice. He has simply discovered that he will not survive if he chooses to do evil.

If human beings were programmed to be unable to do wrong, or if the universe automatically punished evil, there could be no ethical decisions to make. Humans would of necessity have to follow a design built into them, as a clock is made to keep correct time; it has no choice. The possibility of goodness can only exist while the possibility for evil exists. If there is to be a Universe in which genuine goodness can develop, it must also be one in which terrible evil can emerge. Only if there is real freedom to choose can there be goodness; only if evil is an option can goodness be a reality. The Universe is morally neutral. Ultimate Reality includes those moral opposites that matter so deeply, and we are given freedom to make choices.

Is God Pure Love?

In his book *Healing Words*, Larry Dossey, M.D., observes that there is a prevalent idea these days that when we recognize our true spiritual nature we shall be always happy. A few human beings seem to have achieved that state. But many of the spiritual masters hold that God is not pure bliss or pure love or pure anything. These masters maintain that God is unknowable and indefinable because if we say that the ultimate is purely any quality, then we exclude the opposite quality. However, since nothing can exist outside the ultimate, the ultimate must include opposite qualities.

Dossey cites the thirteenth-century Christian mystic Meister Eckhart, who wrote that some people want to recognize God only in some pleasant enlightenment—but then they may get pleasure and enlightenment, but not God.[44] Even so, it is widely accepted that love is redemptive. When the human situation becomes tense, or conflicted, or confused, a loving relationship may be able to help straighten it out. A person who feels lonely or abandoned does not feel quite so lost if love enters the situation. Even the accepting attitude of a counselor who allows the client to feel and to say what is really within him shows that acceptance can open doors for healing. The Christian experience demonstrates a conviction that God's love enables people to get a fresh start in life. Such accepting love empowers people to be honest, to face their shadow side, to develop honesty as they look at themselves in the world, including their imperfection.

The experience of being loved fosters a sense of self-value—"someone loves me, and therefore I am valuable." Of course, other things are also needed: the sense of justice, of belonging, of having a way to participate. If we feel that the universe accepts us, we feel a growing confidence to accept our role in it. We know that the flow of energies around us—the currents of love or of hate—can either sustain or destroy us. Love is a positive power in people's lives. So, ambiguous as it is, the universe contains healing resources that we are able to receive and to use, even as our bodies contain a power of life to heal wounds, along with a strong urge to strive for life.

Creativity flows from an aspect of love that the Greeks called *eros*, which is the desire or need for something or someone other than oneself. It is expressed in sexuality and in the need for relationship. Old myths say that everything came into being because the Ultimate Oneness of the empty void wanted something to relate to—something other than the emptiness. Modern physics curiously echoes this idea. In an earlier chapter we quoted the words of Fritjof Capra: "A careful analysis . . . shows that the subatomic particles have no meaning as isolated entities but can be understood only as interconnections, or correlations, between various processes of observation and measurement."[45]   Relationships, interconnectedness, and cosmic correlations are essential. *Eros* is a drive for connectedness. Ultimate Reality includes *eros*, the primal creativity. Love as *eros* is in the ongoing processes of the cosmos. It is a given, along with existence.

There is yet another dimension of love to be considered. In the Hebrew Bible, the writers affirm that the release of the Hebrews from slavery in Egypt is a gesture of God's love, that God chose Israel out of love, and that God gave the Torah as a mark of love. Many prophets affirmed that even though the chosen people did not keep their part of the covenant with God, God continued to love them.

In the New Testament, the Greek word *agape* was used to describe God's selfless love for the world. Metaphors of human love are used all through the Bible to try to clarify God's love for the people; he is compared to a loving husband, a devoted father, a nurturing mother. The New Testament writers describe the obligations of believers in Christ to treat each other in a selfless way. In other words, such love is seen as *something we can choose*. Jesus said that the sum of human goodness is to "...love God with all your heart, and love your neighbor as yourself."

Metaphors are helpful, but it is important to remember that metaphors are *human* attempts to put forth *human* ideas about Ultimate Reality. They are *not revelation*—not a deliberately chosen divine self-disclosure. Rather they are *interpretation*—human beings' attempts to share their own vision of the nature of God. The metaphor is, "Just as we love and forgive one another, God also loves and forgives." These ideas of God as selfless love continue to motivate people to live and to think in certain ways.

Let us look again at the human concepts of *up* and *down*. These are real meanings, but as we have seen, they are localized. They apply to the earth but not to the cosmos as a whole. So also, the idea of God as totally selfless love (*agape*) can be seen as a *human idea that changes human behavior*, not as a natural law such as gravity, the speed of light, or $E=mc^2$. This idea of God's love indeed does influence events in the world and it can gradually modify human behavior.

As we try to work on *nonrevealed* theology (a human attempt to think about Ultimate Reality by looking honestly at reality), it is sometimes difficult to make *agape* fit with other things we know about the Universe. But we can see *agape* as a real, though localized part of reality, and it is profoundly interrelated with the human vision of the Universe.

Dr. M. Scott Peck, in his fine book *The Road Less Traveled*, discusses some of the evidence that there are powers of good and love at work in the Universe—powers that enter into our lives unasked. They may arise from within our subconscious mind, or they may come in from external events that impinge on us. He points out that we know a great deal of why psychological and physical disorders arise. Yet, as psychiatrists look into the lives of their patients, who bear the scars of psychic or physical traumas, they marvel that their neuroses are not more severe. Peck concludes that there is a force that we do not fully understand, which seems to operate routinely and fosters mental health even in adverse circumstances. [46]

In a section of his book entitled "Grace," he points out that we are constantly receiving undeserved, unearned, and unexplained benefits and blessings. The human mind and its abilities are amazing, but Dr. Peck notes that even our most sophisticated models of the human mind leave many questions unanswered. He concludes that the mind, despite claiming to believe that there is no such thing as a miracle, is itself a miracle. [47] Dr. Peck's book is an excellent resource for anyone who wishes to explore these ideas more deeply.

Hope for Overcoming Evil

Perhaps the most important thing is to remember that we are not hopeless. The Universe does not just produce pains and calamities. It also provides ways whereby we can share the energies of love, which enable us to confront negative energies. We can choose agape. We can think loving thoughts and can focus good intentions on people around us. We can respond when friends and loved ones wish us well and want good for us. Countless people have been sustained in time of grief or disaster as they become aware of the loving concern of family members and friends, and even strangers in faraway lands. We can also hold others in our hearts and minds with love. This produces what we call encouragement, literally "putting in heart." To take heart means to decide to continue, to decide to act. We decide to go on living, to refuse to give up. We continue to oppose evil as best we can, and this may at times include the use of force.

We bet our lives on the highest well we know. We live in ambiguity, but we are not powerless. As the great universe provides the powers within our bodies that urge us toward health and healing, so also it provides us humans with the freedom to tap the power of *agape* love, which moves us toward healing in our social lives. To decide for good and for love is to decide against hate. Love can change the course of events and keep evil at bay. Because human choices—not some external devil—produce evil, human choices can reduce or control evil. It is really up to us.

The Ends

I once saw a cartoon in which two young girls sit on a bench, a length of twine stretched between them. One of them asks, "Why does a piece of string have two ends but no beginning?"

Obviously, this book has a beginning, but we have come to the place where we are starting to stop or beginning to end (another paradox?). We are coming into not one end, but three.

First, we will gather up loose ends. The image in this common phrase is that of cleaning up disconnected but related pieces. We can gather up loose ends in order to trace the strands of string and wind them up on a spool. Or we might think of weaving a sash or stole that is almost complete; just the loose ends of the long fibers need to be gathered and woven into the fabric. Whatever the image, we will gather together some important strands without which the book would be incomplete. They are too important to leave out of our "theology," but all of them have been the central theme of many books. Our loose ends are a perspective on Jesus, some thoughts about prayer, and a consideration of churches.

The next "end" we look at is death. Death is a fact of life, and we all must face it; but is death *the* end? Many people think so. Many others, however, hold that death is not the end of life, but rather a transformation or metamorphosis. Nobody really knows the answer to this age-old riddle, but many have strong opinions, and there are pieces of evidence to which we should pay special notice. That will take us to the Book End, but we are not yet there.

Loose Ends

The first of our loose ends is the question, "Who and what was Jesus of Nazareth?" Jesus is by far the predominant figure in America's religious life, and any person who professes an interest in religion must be able to have some judgment about Jesus, who is often called Christ.

Christ is not the name of a person but the designation of a function or an office, which in Hebrew was called the *Messiah* ("anointed by God"). *Jesus* is a transliteration of the Greek name *Iasous,* an attempt to render into Greek the Jewish name of the man from Nazareth, which was something like Yeshua or Yehoshua; nobody knows for sure.

In any case, we must consider with honesty and respect the identity of this great figure, Jesus. Who was he? Again, I affirm that *there is no one answer;* each person must answer that question in the way that makes sense to himself. Human responses to Jesus vary all the way from the affirmation that he was God embodied in human flesh, through the declaration that he was a person fully dedicated to the reality of God, to the idea that he was insane and deluded about his identity. These ideas move in different directions, partly because there are vastly different understandings about the writings from which people get their information.

To make sense of this conflict, doubters need some alternative sources of both information and interpretation. One good source for the searcher is Huston Smith's fine book, *The Illustrated Book of World Religions.* Smith, a respected authority on world religions, is a member of the Methodist Church. He also practices the meditation of Buddhists, the prayer rituals of Muslims, and participates in the Jewish festivals of the family into which his daughter married. He sees the value of traditions from many spiritual practices. He speaks of the various religions as "the world's wisdom traditions," and honors the sincere devotion to be found in all of them. His book is an excellent resource for anyone who wishes to understand the deepest roots of the great religious traditions, presented fairly and clearly by someone who values them.

Smith highlights such meager information as we have about Jesus.

He says that, to state it in a minimal way, Jesus was a charismatic healer from a tradition that stretches back to early Jewish history. Jewish seers mediated between the everyday world and the world of Spirit that enveloped it. They drew power from the world of Spirit in order to both challenge and help people.[48]

Smith desires to give full respect to the world's religious traditions, not reducing any of them to superstition or ignorance. He points out that Jesus' followers changed from being afraid of the power of Rome and the authority of the religious leaders of Judaism to being public witnesses to their conviction that Jesus had been raised from death and had entered into a different mode of living. Out of that small group emerged a movement that eventually became the Christian Church. The early church could not say what specifically happened (the information in each of the gospel accounts is different, and they are all different from such information as we get from the letters of St. Paul), but obviously the church was convinced that Jesus' presence was still with them. Smith recognizes these difficulties and avoids the too-simple solution of literalism.

The contradictory accounts in the writings that we now call the New Testament cannot all be literally true. We know that some of the information in the gospels comes from the life and teaching of Jesus, but much of it is based on the various ideas that prevailed in the various local churches, which had become Gentile, not Jewish, institutions.

This is a pervasive difficulty as we seek to understand Jesus. There are very few reliable sources aside from the Bible. One exception is the *Gospel of Thomas,* from the Gnostic tradition, which was written about the same time as the last books of the New Testament. It adds a somewhat different perspective to the canonical accounts. Also, we have a considerable amount of archaeological evidence about the area and time in which Jesus lived, but essentially, we must rely on the New Testament.

Part of the problem is that the gospel accounts emerged from different sources. Some of the information originated with Jesus himself, and part of it grew out of the varying views of young churches that were establishing themselves among the Gentiles in cities of the Roman Empire. In many instances, these strands are hard to distinguish from one another; we know that the perceptions of Jesus changed from area to area of the ancient world and that they were modified through time. It is important to remember the churches themselves wrote and preserved the accounts about Jesus. The written gospels did not produce the church; rather, the gospels grew out of the church.

A group of some eighty Protestant and Roman Catholic scholars calling themselves the Jesus Seminar have been trying to sort out these threads. They are specialists, competent in the Greek language in which the New Testament books were written, and in the history, sociology, and politics of Jesus' time. They meet at intervals to discuss and vote on the authenticity of passages under consideration. They seek to answer a fundamental question: Do these passages represent authentic statements of Jesus, or do they come from the opinions of the churches in which the writers were at home?

The seminar has made much progress, but nobody *knows* exactly whether the judgment of these fine scholars is correct or not. However, their work provides a solid basis for people who seriously wish to explore the differences between Jesus' teachings and the teaching of the church about him.

One seminar member, Marcus Borg, has written an especially helpful book, *Meeting Jesus Again, for the First Time.*[49] Borg is a professor in the Department of Religion at Oregon State University. He recounts his own faith odyssey, from a boy who accepted all teachings about Jesus as equally true, to a young man who thought they were essentially too conflicted to be true. He finally became a mature scholar as well as a loyal disciple of the Jesus whose character emerges from the work of the Jesus Seminar. He sees Jesus as a spirit-filled man who was deeply attuned to the reality of God and who took exception to the social system permeating the Jewish society of his time. The book is an excellent resource for people who desire an honest and scholarly treatment of the character and teachings of Jesus.

For me personally, as a faithful agnostic, I find Borg's portrait of Jesus inspiring and persuasive. Not a divine being disguised in human flesh, but a being fully human in all respects, Jesus was a critic of the purity system that dominated Jewish society in his day. Purity systems in any society divide the world between the pure ("the clean"), and the impure ("the unclean"). The poor often could not afford the practices and demands of purity, so they became impure, unclean, left out. Jesus ministered to the poor, the unclean, the impure. He declared God's love and acceptance of these left-out people.

The portrait of the Jesus we meet "again for the first time" in Borg's book is not "gentle Jesus, meek and mild," but a courageous person, strong of spirit, fully dedicated to his ideals, and filled with awareness of a compassionate and caring God. In this awareness, he confronted his society and paid the not unexpected penalty of death. Borg's portrait brings new life and power to the man who is often buried beneath the dead letter of orthodox dogma.

Prayer—a Meaningless Anachronism?

Prayer, of course, has been a part of spiritual practice since there has been any spiritual practice. I would guess that some sort of prayer— the attempt to communicate with the gods—was the first form of religious ritual. In any case, prayer has a very long history. It began when the human world was filled with spirits—in rivers and springs, in trees and caves, in great boulders and cloud-capped mountains. Gods spoke through thunderstorms and wandered among the stars. People were steeped in awareness of the divine.

Our view of the universe has changed, and we now know that we live on a small planet circling a medium-size star in a universe containing billions of galaxies and multiplied billions of stars. As we consider these unfathomable reaches of space and incomprehensible lengths of time, many of us question whether prayer is more than a living fossil.

Yet vestiges of prayer emerge at times of crisis or amid experiences of awful splendor. An airplane suddenly drops several hundred feet in an unexpected downdraft, and startled passengers of all faiths—and no faith—scream the ancient syllable that symbolizes divine power.   A few years ago, Nancy and I took a leisurely June motor trip through Canada. We wanted to see Mt. Robson, the highest peak in the Canadian Rockies, and we were on the highway that climbed alongside the Fraser River, flowing in a deep, shaded valley with steep mountains and foothills on both sides. There was no clear view of the great peaks because the nearby elevations blocked the distant scene. Once in a while we could glimpse sunlight on slopes higher than we were, but mostly we enjoyed the forested ridges and valleys near at hand. Then, as we rounded a sharp curve, suddenly there it was—the magnificent towering cliffs of Mt. Robson.

The clouds that gathered about its peak gleamed with sunshine reflected from the mountain's snowy slopes, as though some giant spotlight were focused on it. From our viewpoint, still in deep shadow near the base of the mountain, we gazed in wonder at the upward thrust of rocky cliffs and terraces.

"Oh, my God!" said Nancy.

We felt that we were indeed in the presence of the Mystery of powerful forces and ancient days and visions of the sacred. Kahlil Gibran writes in *The Prophet,* "You pray in your distress and in your need; would that you might pray also in the fullness of your joy and in your days of abundance." Were Nancy's words a prayer? At the very least, they were a spontaneous expression of a deeply spiritual experience, a profound connection with the universe.

We moderns have absorbed Ambrose Bierce's cynical definition of prayer: "To ask that the rules of the universe be annulled on behalf of a single petitioner, confessedly unworthy." Too often we dismiss prayer as a way of begging God to do something special for us; we tend to think somehow that God listens and then decides whether or not to respond. He then may grant the wish (if we are good enough, if we beg hard enough, if we have the correct set of beliefs). On the other hand, he may not respond, and we have no way of knowing why.

If prayer is not seen as groveling to persuade the Creator to change the order of the universe, but rather as a communication of our real selves, then it can be an expression of gratitude or appreciation, or a spontaneous cry of fear or hurt, or a shout of joy. It does not have to be addressed to any specific destination. ("To God, from Joe. Please expedite handling.") We can be grateful without being grateful to any specific entity.

However, prayer may indeed be an expression of concern for someone who is ill or in pain. Then the question becomes, does prayer work? Is it honest? Can one be scientifically grounded and yet pray with integrity?

Larry Dossey, M.D., reports an enormous body of scientific evidence that prayer can bring about significant changes in a variety of living things. This, he says, surprised him. He tells how he changed from a youth who believed thoroughly in a fundamentalist religion to a skeptical college student and finally to a mature medical doctor who renewed his spiritual life with ideas from many sources. He began to research the evidence reported in scientific studies on the effectiveness of prayer. He summarizes these findings in two books, *Healing Words* (1993) and *Prayer is Good Medicine* (1996). Dossey cites a number of scientific studies on prayer-based psychic healing. Over half of those showed statistically significant results, and there are nearly 150 experiments with living creatures in which telepathy apparently influenced their behavior in various ways.[50]

Dossey points out that prayer can take many forms; often it is not even consciously expressed. People who simply prayed, "May the best result happen," had as many positive results as people who prayed for specific outcomes.[51] He addresses the question of what specific belief systems a person must have in order to pray effectively. His answer? None.

Prayer is basically communication with the Absolute, and people can define both the Absolute and communication in their own ways. Some see the Absolute as transcendent ("out there") and others as immanent ("in here"). The particular theological system of the person who prays is not significant.[52] There is no indication that conservative Christians are more capable at prayer than Reform Jews or High Church Episcopalians or Buddhists. Some do not visualize God as personal; some are drawn to a sense of universal order and majesty.[53]

My brief summary does small justice to Dossey's careful work. He not only includes the evidence that supports the effectiveness of prayer, he also points out the evidence that allows a skeptical response. He clearly acknowledges that prayer is not always effective. He admits that researchers face difficult problems in applying scientific research to nonscientific matters. Nevertheless, he believes that medical practice will increasingly acknowledge the importance of spiritual—or psychic—influences. Dossey's thoughtful works raise important questions for the skeptic and provide many significant answers for the sincere searcher.

Prayer is no substitute for action, especially medical action. Nevertheless, if we are aware of our connectedness with the universe, we can use that connection as a reminder that no event is isolated from all other events. And if we think of the universe in terms of Sir James Jeans' statement that it is more like a great thought than a great machine, our own thoughts and intentions for the world are part of that great universal thought.[54]

Churches: Useful or Harmful?

Many people say that they believe in God, but they do not like organized religion. I can appreciate that position. All too often the rules of the organization predominate and guide the life of the churches. We are left with the impression that the organization exists for the sake of the rules, not for the sake of its members. The central rule is, "The rules must be followed. Period."

So, is a church necessary?

The brief (but incomplete) answer is "No." People can live their entire lives and never set foot inside a church, temple, mosque, or synagogue. Not only that, but they can be upright, moral people, thoughtful people with deep convictions. However, this does not mean that religious institutions have no meaning or purpose. Even for people who have rejected all dogma and doctrine, belonging to such a group serves several needs.

For example, if we believe in the basic principle of individual freedom and responsibility, we give power to that ideal by linking ourselves with others who share it. A lone individual has little chance of advancing any idea unless she can convince other people to join in. In a paradoxical way, if we oppose the power of entrenched institutions, it is important to be part of an institution that also opposes too much institutional power. To say it again another way, if we espouse any real hopes for a society with open spiritual attitudes, we need to embody such hopes in a group of open-minded people.

Second, if we participate in a group that not only searches for its own truth but also believes that such a search is important for others, we become part of a community. In general, our species does not live as isolated individuals; hermits and recluses are a rarity. We gather in cities and towns and we form groups for various reasons:

- We *learn* how to live with others.

- We gather to *play* games with each other, or to watch others playing.

- We *work* to produce different things for our economy, so that every person doesn't have to perform every task that is needed by the larger community.

- We *explore ideas, work for causes,* and *seek ways of governing* ourselves.

Schools and sports teams, banks and factories, churches and synagogues, even political parties all have places in our lives. Our larger human community contains multitudes of small communities. A religious community can provide a sense of belonging; its members can (and do) provide support for each other in time of sorrow and trouble. They reinforce each other's ideas. They seek to embody their ideals in a sometimes hostile world, and they learn from the perceptions and reasoning of others. An open group enables people to grow.

Sometimes, people are critical because early Christians modified and expanded accounts of the teachings of Jesus and embellished his deeds with their own impressions of what they thought he *should* have been. Yet, the critics often forget that we would not have *any* knowledge of Jesus or his teachings if groups had not preserved and handed down the traditions. That is precisely the nature of the world we live in; we could not be where we are had it not been for those ancestors with whom we disagree!

If a person wishes to explore the possibility of finding a compatible spiritual group, he should carefully look for certain denominations and individual congregations that encourage their members to think, question, and grow intellectually as well as spiritually. Such a group may be of real help to the honest skeptic, provided that it embodies those values that the searcher holds—honesty, openness to all aspects of truth, lack of bigotry, and respect for human integrity.

Death: *the End?*

Death is the ultimate fact of life. Life is the absolutely necessary precondition for death. No one has ever died who has not previously lived, and we know of nobody who has lived whose life has not ended in death. We tend to picture death as a patient stalker, following us invisibly all the days of our years, his scythe at the ready for a vulnerable moment. His black robe is loosely draped over a skeleton, and within the hood, a grinning skull peers eyelessly, watching and waiting. The Book of Job calls him "the King of Terrors," and the Roman poet Horace writes, "Pale Death, with impartial step, knocks at the poor man's cottage and at the palaces of kings."

However, this common picture is totally false—death does not exist. I do not mean that death is not real. Everywhere in the world we find beings who have died and are dying. We see the processes of life proceeding toward their end, but there is no thing that bears the name Death and skulks in shadows like a determined and ruthless assassin. Death is our name for the end of the life process, and often we welcome it when we struggle with the deteriorating apparatus of the flesh or long for release from our prison of physical helplessness. Sometimes, however, we face death before we have even lived. Sometimes a young man, a young woman, must leave loved and loving parents, partners, or dependent children. All too often, death means aching hearts and flowing tears, lonely days and even lonelier nights. So death is real, and often it is painful. But is it the end?

Human beings have always been sharply divided about this issue. The great Indian epic *Mahabarata* (from the fourth or fifth century BCE) says, "Possessed by delusion, a man toils for his wife and child; but whether he fulfills his purpose or not, he must surrender the enjoyment thereof. When one is blessed with children and flocks and his heart is clinging to them, Death carries him away as doth a tiger a sleeping deer."

Epicurus (around 300 BCE) writes, "Death is nothing to us, since when we are, death has not come, and when death has come, we are not."

The Buddhist *Dhammapada* (also around 300 BCE) says, "The body dies but the spirit is not entombed."

Finally, the Muslim Al-Ghazzali (about 1100 CE) says, "The meaning of death is not the annihilation of the spirit, but its separation from the body, and the resurrection and day of assembly do not mean a return to a new existence after annihilation, but the bestowal of a new form of frame to the spirit."

So, how can we approach this ultimate portion of earthly life, we who live in a world filled with scientific accomplishments and dominated by scientific understanding? Intellectual integrity demands that we be honest with ourselves and that we do not try to squeeze ourselves into some popular pattern of thought that does not fit our minds. Aware of the inevitability of our own death and that of the people we love, we face life with appreciation for the gifts that are ours.

Even if we are truly committed to the idea that there is life beyond this life, separation from loved ones brings sorrow and a certain emptiness. If we knew that a beloved person was moving away to another part of the world and that we would never see him again, his departure and absence would cause pain. So in any case, as we face inevitable separation, we learn to value the gifts of love, sharing, and tenderness. We enrich our lives and feel gratitude for what we experience, no matter our opinion about life after death.

In my early years of ministry, I was never comfortable assuring people that they would meet again with their dead loved ones. I could repeat the words, but I doubted that I was much comfort to the bereaved. I *could* share their pain, and I could empathize with their loneliness and sense of loss. I know by experience that expressions of sympathy and shared sorrow really do help.

Then there followed in my life an interlude outside any kind of church work, and when I finally began to participate again in the life of a congregation, I had concluded that our life ends when we die. Period. I felt no need to try to convince anyone that they would see their loved ones again. We shared memories and appreciation for the dead and honored the lives they had lived. We remembered what love they had shared, what gifts they had brought. (On the somewhat rare occasions nowadays when I conduct a memorial service, that is still the general procedure I follow. A memorial service is to celebrate the life and to mourn the person who has died; it is not for philosophizing about what happens after death or trying to convince people that they should "believe and not grieve.")

Somewhere, though, about twenty years in the past, some new thoughts began for me. I realized that the boundaries between living and nonliving are vague and changeable. I realized, for example, that the face of a stone cliff gradually wears away through time. Water slowly erodes atoms of the stone; iron, perhaps, or zinc or calcium. Whatever they are, the nonliving minerals in the cliff are washed away by the rains and become part of the water, the streambed.

Downstream, tiny bits of matter from the dead cliff become part of the soil at the edge of the stream. Rootlets of plants spread into the damp soils, and the particles of mineral are incorporated into living plants. The nonliving atoms become part of living tissue, helping to build the leaves or stem of the plant. What had been nonliving in the cliff is now alive in a plant.

In time, a rabbit eats the plant, and the atoms from the cliff become part of the flesh of the rabbit. The rabbit dies and its body decays; again the atoms are not alive. And so the atoms go, moving between the living and nonliving, between plants and worms and grass and cattle, until one day a human being eats a hamburger and they become part of a human body. Now, as I write, those lifeless atoms from the cliff face are part of my own living system, and they participate in my effort to put these words on paper.

The universe is the first recycler. Ancient stars, by their self-destruction, provide the elements that become planets and all their subparts, including cliffs and continents, bacteria and people. The long cycles of movement between living and nonliving mean that context must be considered when we try to judge whether matter is alive.

That is not all, however. About the time that I perceived the dynamic dance of atoms and molecules moving between life and death, I encountered for the first time stories of near-death experiences (NDEs). I began to understand that not only are the boundaries between living and nonliving vague and variable, but that the boundaries between life and death are also vague and variable, that sometimes it is very hard to judge whether the tide of individual life is still flowing or whether it has ceased. Reports of NDEs came from trustworthy and careful observers; they encompassed people of all ages, religious beliefs, and diverse circumstances. Some happened in hospitals and others involved accidents and even attempted suicide.

I asked myself why I should trust the accounts of Elisabeth Kübler-Ross when she reported on the actual processes of dying, but found myself in outright disbelief as she described incidents of NDE. Since then, I have done much reading about NDEs; there seems to be no disagreement that these events happen. The disagreement is about their meaning. Some intelligent people see them as evidence of another dimension of life beyond death. Others hold they are merely a physiological reaction as the body's functions shut down.

As for me, I do not know the answer, but I believe that there is good (but not final) evidence that NDEs point toward some sort of life beyond the boundary we call death. We cannot dismiss the phenomenon simply because we do not yet understand it fully.

Larry Dossey quotes psychologist Abraham Maslow:

If there is any primary rule of science, it is . . . acceptance of the obligation to acknowledge and describe all of reality, all that exists, everything that is the case . . . It must accept within its jurisdiction even that which it cannot understand, explain, that for which no theory exists, that which cannot be measured, predicted, controlled, or ordered . . . It includes all levels or stages of knowledge, including the inchoate, . . . knowledge of low reliability . . . and subjective experience.[55]

A new book, entitled in a manner that might cause anxiety to a serious searcher, actually provides an excellent and comprehensive source to learn what is now known about NDEs: *The Complete Idiot's Guide to Near Death Experiences.*[56] Recommended among book reviews in the Institute of Noetic Sciences *Review*, its nearly

450 pages give a history of modern findings about NDEs and present arguments both for and against seeing these experiences as insights into a higher dimension. The book provides a thorough listing of books and resources, including e-mail addresses, for those who wish to pursue this topic.

There is yet another perspective on the universe as the great recycler; it is somewhat akin to the idea that small bits of matter are constantly recycled through different kinds of living and nonliving systems. I mention now reincarnation, the very old idea that individual souls recycle. The concept of dynamic continuity is prevalent in Hinduism and Buddhism, and though it is not so strong in Western traditions, it has been growing in influence, especially since New Age thought emerged during the 1960s.

There are many possible sources for the searcher who wishes to explore evidence for reincarnation or rebirth. A major researcher in this field is Ian Stevenson, M.D., professor of psychiatry and personality studies at the University of Virginia. His valuable books are available in libraries and bookstores.

A book by another psychiatrist, Brian L. Weiss, M.D., stirred my mind to the point of saying, "This book convinces me that this whole set of ideas must be taken seriously!" Written clearly and persuasively, Weiss's book recounts his unexpected experience as he hypnotically regressed a young patient back to childhood (seeking a clue to her persistent personal difficulties). To his surprise, she began speaking of a completely different life in a different place and time.

Later, Weiss's patient gave him information about his own family that he had never told anyone. His experience convinced him of the authenticity of what she was reporting, and he finally shared it in this book, though he knew that its publication might damage his professional reputation. I do not know what the full meaning of it all might be, but I believe that this book reports a reality that I did not expect, do not understand, and cannot ignore. The book is *Many Lives, Many Masters,* by Brian Weiss, M.D.[57]

So is death *the* end? Maybe, but contrary to what I would have said some twenty years ago, my bet is, probably not.

The Book End

There is an old saying that the task of the minister is to "comfort the afflicted and afflict the comfortable." In other words, the task is to soothe the disturbed and shake up the complacent. It is to add a dimension to people's lives. In a certain sense, this has been my procedure in writing this book. I hoped to add a sense of the possibility of spirit to the mind that is centered on science, and to suggest a serious appreciation for the scientific disciplines for the mind that dwells in spirit. As humans we need both; we are neither disembodied spirits nor merely complicated lumps of meat, and in the realms of both science and spirit there are intermingled mysteries that surround us. We are intelligent, but there is much that we do not know.

Living in both worlds allows us to grow, to experience both realms, and to live by reason and faith by betting our lives on our ultimate commitment. Like all human beings, we will not know the final answers unless and until we perhaps find out by experience. What we shall find out at the last may be that we really don't know as much as we think we do.

I close this book with a prayer, though I cannot tell you exactly to whom it is addressed. It is an expression of sincere but limited aspiration, written in the belief that Ultimate Reality includes the qualities we need to enrich our human lives and honor our human search. It is written in profound appreciation for all my friends who have prodded me into thinking more deeply than was sometimes comfortable: for Mark and Janice, for Jeremy and Meg, and Julia and Sam, and all seekers, whoever and wherever you are.

Great Mystery, of whom we are also a small and mysterious part, we are grateful for those creative mysteries of life and love and hope. We worship not what we know, but what we do not know, for our knowledge disappears into the great circle of the invisible. Out of the vast unknown, out of the powers that we can but faintly imagine, out of the circle of bright darkness beyond our ken, we have come together. We are not called by you to assemble ourselves. We assemble ourselves because we seek to understand who we are; we worship the worth-ship of the universe.

May we live with compassion among our fellow beings, with

our patchy glimpses of relationship in the mystery of which we are part. Sometimes we wander, not knowing where we are nor where we go, and sometimes we are fearful. Sometimes the mysteries of life and death shimmer in the circle of reality just beyond our vision. May we trust those doubts that urge us to open our minds to new understandings. May we learn how to strengthen and comfort one another. May we live fully and rejoice in our physical creaturehood; and may we take courage from persistent hints of spirit.

May we share the bread of life, the warmth of love, and the challenges of freedom that empower us to do good and to do evil. May we have wisdom to choose well, for the benefit of our world and of the fragile societies of which we are part. And may we be graced with courage and honesty to seek reality and strength in our living, and tender care in our relationships with each other. And may we be ready to receive rare visions of that which transcends our mundane lives and revitalizes our spirits.

So may it be!

NOTES

Introduction

1. John Shelby Spong, *Here I Stand* (San Francisco: Harper-SanFrancisco, 2000), 74.

CHAPTER ONE: *The Case of the Faithful Agnostic*

2. Paul Tillich, *Dynamics of Faith* (New York: Harper and Brothers, 1957), 1.

3. Edward Harrison, *Masks of the Universe* (New York: Collier Books, Macmillan, 1985), 197.

4. John Horgan, *The End of Science: Facing the Limits of Knowledge in the Twilight of the Scientific Age* (Reading, MA: Helix Books, Addison-Wesley Publishing Company, Inc., 1996), 8.

CHAPTER THREE: *Kite String and the Web of Interdependence*

5. Tillich, 75.

6. Ibid., 76.

7. Joseph Wood Krutch, *The Measure of Man* (Gloucester, MA: Peter Smith Publisher, Inc., 1978), 138.

8. Horgan, 111.

9. Fritjof Capra, *The Tao of Physics* (Boston: Shambhala Publications, 1975), 57.

CHAPTER FOUR: *Personal Faith in a God That Does Not Exist*

10. Tillich, quoted in Charles P. Curtis and Ferris Greenslet, *The Practical Cogitator, or The Thinker's Anthology* (Boston: Houghton Mifflin Company, 1962), 595.

11. James Hillman, *The Soul's Code: In Search of Character and Calling* (New York: Random House, 1996), 95.

12. Robert Ellsberg, ed., *Gandhi on Christianity* (Maryknoll, NY: Orbis Books, 1991), 62.

CHAPTER FIVE: *Thinking About the Unthinkable*

13. Einstein, quoted in Harrison, *Masks of the Universe*, 57.

14. Harrison, 123.

15. Gerhard Staghun, *God's Laughter: Man and His Cosmos* (New York: Aaron Asher Books, Harper Collins Publishers, 1992), 141.

16. Fritjof Capra, *The Turning Point: Science, Society, and the Rising Culture* (New York: Simon & Schuster, 1982), 77, 78.

17. Capra, *The Tao of Physics*, 124.

18. Ibid., 188.

19. Sir James Jeans and David Bohm are discussed in Capra, *The Turning Point*, 86.

20. Benjamin Whorf, *Language, Thought, and Reality* (New York: The Technology Press of Massachusetts Institute of Technology with John Wiley and Sons, 1956), 85.

21. Harrison, 270, 271.

22. Joseph Campbell with Bill Moyers, *The Power of Myth* (New York: Doubleday, 1988), 12, 13.

23. Harrison, 268.

24. Ibid., 271.

25. Ibid., 272.

26. Campbell, 31.

27. Ibid., 32.

CHAPTER SIX: *The Meaning and Myth of Being Human*

28. Tillich, 50.

29. These ideas are developed in Tillich, 41ff.

30. Tillich, 51, 52.

31. Colin Tudge, *The Time Before History: Five Million Years of Human Impact* (New York: Scribner, 1996), 23.

32. Ibid., 24, 25.

33. Lewis Thomas, *A Long Line of Cells* (New York: Book-of-the-Month Club, 1990), xi, xii.

34. Fritjof Capra, *The Web of Life: A New Scientific Understanding of Living Systems* (New York: Anchor Books, Doubleday, 1996), 216.

35. Ibid., 244, 245.

36. Krutch, 172.

37. Capra, *The Web of Life*, 296.

CHAPTER SEVEN: *What Difference Does It Make?*

38. Fletcher, Joseph, *Situation Ethics* (Philadelphia: Westminster Press, 1966).

39. Ibid., 18.

40. The apocryphal books were religious writings that, for various reasons, were not included among the canonical scriptures. Most of these books are included in Catholic Bibles and are called "deutero-canonical" books. They are variable in quality and subject matter. *Judith* was apparently written around 130 BCE.

CHAPTER EIGHT: *On Evil and the Devil*

41. John Bowker (ed.), *Oxford Dictionary of World Religions* (New York: Oxford University Press, 1997).

42. Ephesians 6:10 ff.

43. Paula Fredriksen, *From Jesus to Christ: Origins of the New Testament Images of Jesus* (New Haven: Yale University Press, 1988), 11.

44. Larry Dossey, *Healing Words: The Power of Prayer and the Practice of Medicine* (New York: Harper Collins, 1993), 23.

45. Capra, *The Tao of Physics*.

46. M. Scott Peck, *The Road Less Traveled: A New Psychology of Love, Traditional Values, and Spiritual Growth* (New York: Touchstone Books, Simon & Schuster, 1978), 238.

47. Ibid., 253.

CHAPTER NINE: *The Ends*

48. Huston Smith, *The Illustrated World Religions: A Guide to Our Wisdom Traditions* (San Francisco: HarperSanFrancisco, 1986), 206 ff.

49. Marcus Borg, *Meeting Jesus Again for the First Time* (San Francisco: HarperSanFrancisco, 1994).

50. Larry Dossey, *Healing Words*, 200.

51. Ibid., 98–100.

52. Larry Dossey, *Prayer Is Good Medicine: How to Reap the Healing Benefits of Prayer* (San Francisco: HarperSanFrancisco, 1996), 84.

53. Ibid., 82.

54. An invaluable resource for any person who seeks a research organization that combines scientific rigor with a nonreductionist vision of reality is The Institute of Noetic Sciences (475 Gate Five Road, Suite 300, Sausalito, CA 94965). Founded by astronaut Edgar Mitchell after a mystical experience during his return from a trip to the moon, the Institute carries on extensive work in many areas of the reach of the mind. These are reported on extensively in their publications. The website is www.noetic.org.

55. Dossey, *Healing Words*, 169.

56. P. M. H. Atwater, and David H. Morgan, *The Complete Idiot's Guide to Near Death Experiences* (Indianapolis: Alpha Books, Macmillan USA Inc., 2000).

57. Brian L. Weiss, *Many Lives, Many Masters* (New York: A Fireside Book, Simon and Schuster, 1988).

Resources

Books

I have found these books to be especially helpful. Some of them are not in print; others are no longer under the names of publishers who produced my own copies. Most deal with various scientific understandings that impact how we can think of Ultimate Reality.

Ethics

Fletcher, Joseph. *Situation Ethics*. Philadelphia: Westminster Press, 1966. Out of print, but you can find it in libraries. Excellent!

Body, Mind, and Faith

Cousins, Norman. *Head First: The Biology of Hope*. New York: E. P. Dutton, 1989.

Dossey, Larry. *Healing Words: The Power of Prayer and the Practice of Medicine*. New York: Harper Collins, 1993.

———. *Prayer Is Good Medicine: How to Reap the Healing Benefits of Prayer*. San Francisco: HarperSanFrancisco, 1996.

Moyers, Bill. *Healing and the Mind*. New York: Doubleday, 1993.

Science

Capra, Fritjof. *The Tao of Physics: An Exploration of the Parallels between Modern Physics and Eastern Mysticism*. Boston: Shambhala, 1999.

———. *The Turning Point: Science, Society, and the Rising Culture*. New York: Bantam, 1982.

Capra, Fritjof. *The Web of Life: A New Understanding of Living Systems*. New York: Anchor Books, Doubleday, 1996.

Darling, David. *Zen Physics, the Science of Death, the Logic of Reincarnation*. New York: HarperCollins, 1996.

Davies, Paul. *God and the New Physics*. New York: Touchstone, Simon & Schuster, 1984.

Harrison, Edward. *Masks of the Universe*. New York: McGraw Hill, 1985.

Wilber, Ken. *The Marriage of Sense and Soul: Integrating Science and Religion*. New York: Random House, 1998.

Zukav, Gary. *The Dancing Wu Li Masters: An Overview of the New Physics*. New York: Bantam, 1980.

New Ways of Looking at the Universe

Talbott, Michael. *The Holographic Universe*. New York: Harper Collins, 1991.

Watts, Alan. *The Book: On the Taboo against Knowing Who You Are*. New York: Random House, 1966.

———. *Nature, Man, and Woman*. New York: Pantheon (Random House), 1958.

———. *Psychotherapy East and West*. New York: Pantheon (Random House), 1961.

Wilber, Ken. *A Brief History of Everything*. Boston: Shambhala, 1996.

Christianity and Other Religions

Borg, Marcus. *Meeting Jesus Again for the First Time*. San Francisco: HarperSanFrancisco, 1994.

Smith, Huston. *The Illustrated World's Religions: A Guide to Our Wisdom Traditions*. San Francisco: HarperSanFrancisco, 1991.

About the Author

Joseph S. Willis was awarded his Master's Degree in Divinity from Princeton Theological Seminary in 1943, and did doctoral work at the Divinity School of the University of Chicago. After serving various Presbyterian churches in New Jersey, Texas, New Mexico, and Illinois, he became University Pastor at the University of New Mexico, and later worked in the Albuquerque public schools as a teacher and counselor. Since his retirement from the school system, he has served Unitarian churches in New Mexico and Colorado, and is Minister Emeritus at Jefferson Unitarian Church in Golden, Colorado. A professional landscape painter, he lives with his wife, Nancy, in Arvada, Colorado.

QUEST BOOKS
are published by
The Theosophical Society in America,
Wheaton, Illinois 60189-0270,
a branch of a world fellowship,
a membership organization
dedicated to the promotion of the unity of
humanity and the encouragement of the study of
religion, philosophy, and science, to the end that
we may better understand ourselves and our place in
the universe. The Society stands for complete
freedom of individual search and belief.
For further information about its activities,
write, call 1-800-669-1571, e-mail olcott@theosmail.net
or consult its Web page: http://www.theosophical.org

The Theosophical Publishing House
is aided by the generous support of
THE KERN FOUNDATION,
a trust established by Herbert A. Kern
and dedicated to Theosophical education.

PRAISE FOR
FINDING FAITH IN THE FACE OF DOUBT

I like Willis's open-minded approach to a subject clouded by confusing mythology. By honest and intelligent inquiry, he proposes that faith leads to a satisfying understanding of religious issues.
— Edward Harrison, Astronomer, Steward Observatory,
University of Arizona; author of *Masks of the Universe*

In this companionable guide to life's most enduring questions, Willis ennobles doubt by extending its purview, making room for honest faith.
— Forrest Church, Minister, All Souls Unitarian Universalist Church,
New York, NY; author of *Life Craft: The Art of Meaning in the Everyday*

Joe Willis forces us, in an engaging and relaxed way, to confront the fact that behind everything about us there is a mystery, and that to confront that mystery in any meaningful way requires a theology.
— Richard Hansen, Ph.D., Chief Geophysicist;
Pearson, deRidder and Johnson, Inc.; Lakewood, Colorado

Joe Willis writes for the ordinary person who struggles with issues of faith and meaning. Without technical jargon, he sets forth a liberal faith stance that is both intellectually satisfying and emotionally warm.
— Edward L. Henderlite, Minister Emeritus,
First Congregational United Church of Christ, Salem, Oregon

Joe Willis has created a book that dares to be different [and] has given expression to our deepest longings and our most lofty hopes for what responsible religion can claim.
— Charles Schuster, Pastor, United Methodist Church, Arvada, Colorado

Written for people who cannot ignore science and logic but who are also seeking ideals and meaning to guide their living, [the book] offers a gentle and kind discussion about spirit, faith, and scientific thinking.
— William D. Emerson, Mathematics Professor at
Metropolitan State College, Denver

Joe Willis is both mentor and sage who leads us on a steadfast path to the crux of the human dilemma.
— Jim Matera, Professional Investor

Those who wonder if questions and doubts make their faith invalid will find reassurance in this scholarly yet accessible work. It's like talking with a kindly grandfather!
— Kerry Pettis, Teacher and Librarian

Life Beyond Death

Kübler-Ross, Elisabeth. *On Life after Death*. New York: Book-of-the-Month Club, 1992.

Weiss, Brian L. *Many Lives, Many Masters*. New York: A Fireside Book, Simon and Schuster, 1988.

Websites

www.noetic.org. Institute of Noetic Sciences. Nonprofit membership organization that does research and education in consciousness and human potential. Conducts and sponsors research into the workings and powers of the mind, including perceptions, beliefs, attention, intention, and intuition.

www.iras.org. Institute on Religion in an Age of Science, Inc. Nondenominational, independent society that promotes, among other things, "human values and contemporary knowledge in such universal and valid terms that they may be understood by all peoples."

www.aril.org Association for Religion and Intellectual Life. Global network for people of faith and intelligence who are committed to connecting the wisdom of the heart and the life of the mind. Publishes *Cross Currents*, a quarterly magazine. More information found at www.crosscurrents.org.

http://zygoncenter.org/ Zygon Center for Religion and Science (formerly known as Chicago Center for Religion and Science). Provides a place of research and discussion between scientists, theologians, and other scholars on understanding the world and our place in it; relating traditional concerns and beliefs of religion to scientific understandings; and reflecting on how to contribute to the welfare of the human community.